The Truth About Me

A Personal Journey in Healing

Kandi A. Cash

This book is dedicated in memory of my mother
the late Julia Lula Stubbs-Anderson
January 24, 1944 - March 28, 2024
A Legend Indeed

Contents

Foreword

I n a world often marred by brokenness and pain, the journey to healing can seem daunting, if not impossible. Yet, it is a journey that we must all undertake if we are to live the fullness of our true purpose. Kandi Cash, with unwavering faith and raw transparency, invites us into her personal journey of healing—a path she was divinely guided to walk.

In *"The Truth about Me ,"* Kandi reminds us that healing is not just a physical process but a profound spiritual journey that touches every aspect of our being. In John 5, Jesus asks the man at the pool of Bethesda if he wanted to be made whole. This question highlights a truth that many overlook: healing is a choice. It is a choice that requires courage, vulnerability, and a willingness to confront the deep wounds within.

This book is more than a testimony; it is a call to action. As you turn these pages, you will find yourself not just reading about Kandi's experiences but reflecting on your own life. Her words, inspired by the Holy Spirit, are meant to stir something within you—to encourage you to take that first step toward your own healing and the freedom of not being ashamed of your own personal story of pain, disappointments and even failures.

Kandi's obedience to God's command in sharing her journey is a gift to us all. It is a reminder that no matter how deep the hurt, there is hope. No matter how broken we feel, wholeness is within reach. This book is not just for those who have experienced trauma but for anyone seeking to live a life of true freedom and purpose.

So, as you begin this journey through the pages of Kandi's story, I encourage you to open your heart. Allow her words to challenge and inspire you. And most importantly, be willing to answer the question that Jesus asked so long ago: Will you be made whole?

Lequient A Bethel

Introduction

Everyone has a story or stories- a combination of events that worked together to contribute to the 'quilt' of their lives and shaped who they've become. These stories are often untold, and in many cases, for good reasons. The challenge with untold stories, though, is that others never get to see, appreciate or understand the 'whys' and the 'hows' about us. As a result, we are seen through lens that do not reflect who we truly are. This often misleads people and creates a false identity that sometimes becomes so heavy that its weight becomes unsustainable over time, for the person carrying it.

The other challenge with an untold story is that people see the 'finished product' without understanding the process and journey that it took to get there. Telling our stories brings a level of unprecedented freedom, not only for us, but for others. It encourages others to overcome as they learn from our life's lessons and it allows others to see the redemptive work that only God can do, once we yield to the healing process.

This book is my story, one that I almost did not tell, and certainly not one that I wanted to tell. Sitting down one morning, crying out to The Lord in prayer and taking a few moments to listen, I heard Him clearly tell me to give myself a deadline to complete my first book- *The House That Faith Built*- because there was another book that He wanted me to write called – *The Truth About Me*. I must admit that this was not a project that I was particularly excited about, to put it mildly. In fact, I was filled with dread, and not holy fear, just dread for having to journey back through my life's story and then to share it so publicly with the world.

I have often heard it said that if you cannot talk about something, then it still hurts and you are not healed from it. I actually did not even realize that I needed to be healed until a prayer partner mentioned it to me through a Word of Knowledge, and even then, I initially could not think of anything that I needed to be healed from at that time. Boy, was I wrong! When the revelation came, it really came. There were so many things that I had packaged into neat little compartments in my heart and mind that required healing to unravel. The question then for me became how? How do I heal from all of the trauma of my past that I conveniently left behind?

A few days after I started writing this book, I had a dream about an unfinished house that I started building, obviously years prior. The house was being built for so long, as I walked around I saw things that needed to be updated because they were considered dated, due to the length of time that the building was taking to be completed. I recall seeing a bathroom sink that looked like it was from the early 1990s and a bathroom cupboard that was also very old and unfinished. As I walked around the house, I started making mental notes of the renovations that needed to be completed simultaneously as I worked to complete the unfinished work in the house.

The revelation of that dream was in direct relation to my healing journey, and the fact that I was on it for years and it is now time for it to come to full completion. Everything that I needed to do, needed to be quickly wrapped up and completed. I know that this was a warning dream and God was admonishing me to complete my healing journey because He is very intentional in using the broken things of our lives to bring glory to Him and to help to bring healing to others. I also know that He will use this book to help me to bring that long journey to a conclusion.

After I started writing, I listened to a message from my Pastor, Lequient Bethel, and he said something that was so profound. He said "your pain can be a prison or a platform". This spoke directly to my heart. If allowed, our pain can trap us in cycles of hurt that spiral out of control and lead us to a path of destruction, or we can use the pain that we experienced to not only come to a place of healing in our own lives, but also influence and inspire healing in the lives of those around us.

The choice was clear, although, my pain was initially a prison with 'work release' where I would venture out and pretend as if my past did not exist, but in my mind and in my heart, I was still bound by the chains of pain, shame and guilt. I finally made the decision, not only to obey God but in doing so, to turn my pain into a platform.

This book is my story, my journey and it is my prayer that as I peel back the layers of my life, you would journey with me and see the amazing work that God has done in me, and can do in you also., if you allow Him. He has the most uncanny ability to turn what we think are the worst stories into the most beautiful reflections of His love and grace.

As you embark on this journey with me, I ask that you remain open to the ways that The Holy Spirit will bring your own memories to the surface and ask Him to heal these areas as He reveals them. So before we embark on this journey, I would like to open in a word of prayer:

Father,

I love You more than anything and You know my heart concerning this book. This is a walk that I did not want to take, but I know that You have a plan not only for my life but the life of the person reading this right now. My prayer is that You touch the deep places of our lives and those areas where we have not shared with anyone, those wounds that need to be revealed so that You can heal.

Father in our weakness, You are strong. I pray for unprecedented healing and freedom to be the portion of every person who reads this book. May our lives become living testimonies for Your glory and honor. Thank You for healing, delivering, and setting us free.

In Jesus' Might and Matchless Name, I ask these things.

Amen.

Chapter One: The Importance of Identity Formation

A newborn child is a blank slate. Newborns do not come into the world with opinions or preconceived notions. Children are born, however, with physical and spiritual genetic blueprints that cause them to look and sometimes behave like others in their family line. I guess at this point it would be important for me to put in a disclaimer that I am, by no means, a scientist.

That said, it is important to note that the blueprints which impact physical features determine skin color, height and sometimes even weight. The spiritual blueprints however determine battles that the child would have to fight, if the cycles were not previously broken, and hopefully win, to change the blueprint for future generations. Family background plays a significant role in our development, our ideologies, belief systems and habits.

Psalms 51:5 in the Passion Translation says *"Lord, I have been a sinner from birth, from the moment my mother conceived me."* This is the truth of our births, but thanks to the amazing grace and love of God, we can be born again and obtain the righteousness that only Jesus Christ can give us. I do not, however, want to get ahead of myself.

I was born into a relatively stable home, or so I thought, with married parents, both teachers. I was my mother's last child and the only girl with two older brothers. Physically I resembled both of my parents in some aspects, however, even as I was the only girl child, I was also the different one in many, many aspects. This is where my story begins and I feel compelled to tell it as I understood it then and even as I understand it now.

My parents were both teachers who were very committed to their profession. My father was a tall handsome man who was always very easy going and fun to be around. He was always on the go and loved to play dominoes and drink beers. My mother on the other hand, came from a 'Christian' home, so she was less inclined socially. They both came from rather large families. My father had so many siblings, I still struggle to remember the names of all of my aunts and uncles. My mom had six siblings alive at the time of my birth. I was told about three others who died when my mom was a child.

My parents travelled around the family of islands in The Bahamas. As teachers in the seventies, the Government offered many incentives to get teachers to establish themselves in any of the islands outside of the capital where my mom grew up. My first memories as a child were on the island of Grand Bahama and there were several memories that stuck with me.

I remember my primary school principal, Mr. Doyle, a big, tall white man with a full beard. I remember the dresses that my mom made for me, she was really great at sewing. I remembered my sixth birthday and the beautiful homemade cake that she made for me. I also remember my tricycle- it was red, white and blue and I had a matching outfit that I loved to wear each time I rode it.

I also had some darker memories that would later play a bigger role in my life. I recall being deathly afraid of the dark, a fear so real that I would literally awake in the middle of the night and run down the hall, sometimes running into the guard rail around our living room as I sought the refuge of my parents' bedroom in the dark. I never understood the source of that fear, but I carried that with me to my early teenage years and even after.

I also remember an evening that my parents had a loud fight, my mom did not want my dad to go out and he physically tore her clothes off as she tried to stop him from leaving. I did not realize it at the time, or for a long time after, but this was not unusual for them, to have serious disagreements that sometimes ended up in physical altercations. I also remember having a 'boyfriend' who lived across the street from our house. Although this was a very innocent relationship, I do recall that he had a cousin about the same age who was the first person that I remember having inappropriate touches with.

I will pause here to say that sometimes parents are so consumed by what is happening in their own lives that they often miss the opportunities that Satan uses to get to their children. Every person is born with a destiny and purpose and when God's hand is upon a child, the enemy will do all that he can to try to abort the child's destiny from as early an age as possible.

Looking back, I could see that my parents were two very different people, and I am amazed that they even connected the way they did and got married. I suspect though, that this decision was not entirely of their making. Much later I learned that my parents were married just before my older brother was born, and almost four years after my oldest brother was born. In my culture and most certainly with my mother's Christian upbringing, to get pregnant without being married was looked upon with disdain. I suspect that given the fact that this was my mother's second child outside of marriage, there was some external pressure to get married.

Almost four years after their wedding, my mom had me. Before she left the hospital, she took drastic measures to make sure that she did not get pregnant again. While this may seem insignificant, it actually gave me some insight later in life. My mom did not want any other children. As I got older, I understood why. I will share a little more on this later.

My parents' marriage from the outside looked like a match made in heaven, but from the inside, things were far from heavenly. My father struggled with infidelity and he was not shy about this fact. As a matter of fact, it seemed like he attracted women who were proud to be his mistresses, and had no issue making my mother aware of this. For any woman, this would be their worst nightmare. My mother was no different, I know now, that this really hurt her.

Regardless of this, and my father's persistent infidelity even to the extent of having children with other women, my mom chose to stay with him. I am really not sure why, and I can attribute it to the cultural pressures at the time to stay in marriages even if they were failing. Thinking about it, my maternal grandmother did the exact same thing, stayed in a failing marriage, even though my grandfather's mistresses had more children than she did.

This goes right back to my earlier point about generational blueprints. I have to pause to say that regardless of what the blueprint looks like, we do not have to live with this plan, we can choose the truth of God's Word. John 8:31-32 says *"Then said Jesus to those Jews which believed on him, If ye continue in my word, then are ye my disciples indeed; 32and ye shall know the truth, and the truth shall make you free."* **King** James Version. Regardless of our birth circumstances or childhood experiences and traumas, Jesus is able to set us free.

I want to focus initially on my father. Fathers play a critical role in the lives of their children. I am certain that my father loved me as **best as he** knew how, however, I do not think that he was committed to our family as much as he was committed to living his 'best life' and searching for something that he could never find in the arms of another woman. I also believed that he could not give me or our family what he himself never had.

8

He lost his father at an early age by violent means and his mother had so many children, I'm sure that in spite of her best efforts, it was impossible to grieve, remarry, and still focus on all of her children. Societal norms, I'm sure did not help either. At that time there was more of a focus on making ends meet, providing the basic needs rather than lovingly nurture children or pursuing mental and emotional health.

Allow me to digress to science for a moment. In reproduction, the chromosomes contributed by the male determines the gender of the child. As it is in the natural, so it is in the spirit, fathers are an essential part of identity formation. I am parking here for a moment because I would like to raise a few important points.

The first is the fact that there is often an attack in relationships between fathers and children because the way we interact with our natural fathers often plays a key influential role on how we interact with our Heavenly Father. Our parents are spiritual gatekeepers and guardians, a role granted directly by God.

This role carries a heavy responsibility that is often unrealized by many parents. God honors order and rights. He has created fathers to be the head of their wives and children. The authority of a father making declarations over the lives of his children carries serious spiritual weight. While there are some fathers who are aware of this and have taken up the charge to shape their children's identities, there are many others who either are unaware or just refuse to take this on this profound responsibility.

If you are a father, reading this now, pause and think about the awesome power that God has entrusted to you as it relates to identity formation in your children. You have amazing opportunities to spiritually shape your children, and this responsibility should never be taken lightly. One does not have to look hard to see countless examples of the negative impact that missing or abusive fathers can have on the lives of their children.

Well into adulthood, many people still struggle with the challenges that developed in their lives because of fathers who were unaware of the weight of their words and actions on their children's lives or simply just absent. When a father declares words over his child, these words are backed by heaven or hell depending on if these words are of God or not. Either way, they carry weight because of the authority given by God.

Ok, back to my parents. In spite of my father's exploits, I loved him and looked up to him so much. I remember games that he would play with me, and times that he would take me and my siblings, including the ones that I didn't even realize were siblings at the time, to the beach. I am told that he would even take me to his mistress' house, I was too young to remember, however, my mom told me about it when I was older, and I'm sure that did not end very well.

As a young girl, I always felt closer to my dad than I did with my mother, which I thought to be a little strange, given that I was her only daughter and the youngest of their three children. For some reason, I don't even remember feeling really connected to her as a child. As a matter of fact, I don't remember feeling connected to her in the way a daughter should connect with a mother, until much later in life when I started dating the young man who would eventually become my husband.

While I can only guess now why my mother was always so emotionally disconnected, I have a strong suspicion that it was because of the pain that she endured for most of her life at that point and even for years to come- pain that she evidently never faced, or was healed from.

My mother was the second oldest child of six children. She was quite a philosopher. She would tell her children, and all who knew her, many 'sayings' that would leave the hearers of these nuggets of wisdom thinking about her words long after she left their presence. I realized later that many of these sayings were passed down from her parents. Not all of these 'words of wisdom' were good, some of them were and others were not.

One thing I can say though, they provided quite a bit of insight into her upbringing. According to her and her siblings, her father would tell his children that they didn't need friends, and that there were enough of them to be friends with each other. This in my opinion had to have led to some form of loneliness. I recall seeing an old scar on my mother's thigh and her telling me that she received a deep wound on her leg from a nail, while running home so that my grandfather would not find out that she was outside playing with friends.

My mother was a very private person, but on odd occasions, she would open up briefly and talk about how she felt and some of her experiences. When I was sixteen, I found out that my oldest brother was not my father's child. I remember my mom sharing with me, sometime after this 'secret' was out, that before she became pregnant with him, she recalled a friend asking her to be a godparent to her child. The person was not married and she told her friend that she would not be a godmother to an illegitimate child.

She clearly regretted those words as three months later, she found herself pregnant and unmarried. She even went on to say that when she was less than six months pregnant, her child's father went on to marry someone else- my mom at this time was in her early twenties. Almost four years later, she found herself pregnant again, this time, she went to the altar with this child's father. I'm sure that she often thought about how her life turned out to be so different from how she figured it would and I am sure that these thoughts kept her occupied to the extent that having yet another child was not to the forefront of her mind.

It is so important that we allow God in to heal our wounds, otherwise the pain drives deeper and deeper in and before we know it, we are hurting our loved ones, and are unable to explain why. She had clearly experienced rejection over and over in her lifetime and as the saying goes- hurt people hurt people. I will take it a step further and say that rejected people reject people.

She was rejected and as a result we were rejected. This does not mean that she didn't care about her children, or provide for us, she always did, it just became apparent that her pain began to govern her life and the cycle continued- as a result there was always an emotional disconnect.

Children come into the world as blank slates and they are shaped by their environment. It does not matter what your background is, do not allow what happened to you to shape your children. Be deliberate and intentional and pour into them. If you experienced pain, pause and allow God to heal you, to heal that broken little boy or girl- He can, I have experienced it and you can also. We will go into this more in a later chapter.

Chapter Two: Growing Up Quickly

Around 1980, my family moved to New Providence, Bahamas. After years of living on different islands in the Bahama Islands chain. My parents completed the home that they were building and we moved into our newly constructed home. I remember that there were still a few things to be done, like putting down flooring, but it was an exciting time. We had no furniture and we made up beds on top of cardboard on the concrete floor. I remember bit by bit, over time, the rooms began to form into actual bedrooms with furniture in it.

As the only girl, I had the privilege of having my own bedroom. In spite of this, I continued to 'sleep' in my parents' room. I was so afraid of the dark that my parents would have no choice but to allow me to sleep in their bedroom. I remember a little nook between the bed and the wall that I nestled into with my little arm holding on tightly to my mom's waist. What I did not know is that when I was fast asleep my parents would put me in my room to sleep in my bed, and bring me back into their room before I awoke in each morning.

In the Christmas of 1981, my parents sent my siblings and I to another island to spend the holidays with my dad's family. I never knew why, but I do recall how strange it felt to watch others open gifts and not to have gifts of our own, because our gifts were at home. I had no idea how the loneliness that Christmas would play an even bigger role in the days to come. Meanwhile back at home, my mom purchased a black La-Z-Boy chair for my father as a gift, it was a beautiful leather chair that must have cost her a pretty penny on her teacher's salary.

A few weeks later, specifically on January 5, 1982, I woke up for the first time in my bedroom, puzzled, and wondering how I got in my room, when I knew that I went to sleep in my parents' bed. I recall slowly moving out of my room because of unfamiliar noises outside of my bedroom. As I walked down the hallway into the living room, I saw my mother seated in my father's new chair with her face awash in tears, moaning and crying like I had never heard her cry before.

As I continued to try to make sense of what I was seeing, I saw my oldest brother standing next to my mom, he was 15. My other brother was 11 but I don't recall seeing him anywhere. I also recall seeing strangers in our home, in particular a priest, likely my father's priest because my dad was an Anglican, while my mom worshipped at a small southern Baptist church. I remember distinctly how he patted my head.

I also observed a steady stream of people coming in and out of our home, as my mom continued to cry periodically. Only later I would learn that my father was killed in a car crash coming home very early that morning, in the little red Volkswagen Beetle that he drove. He had been out with friends and a large truck ran into him and he did not have a chance. He was taken to the hospital where he later died.

The next few days were a blur, but these series of events played a significant role in my development. As my mom and relatives worked to plan my dad's funeral, I just recall people being in and out of our home, trying to help in any way that they could. My father, whom I loved so much and I felt so close to, was snatched away from me, and in my seven-year old mind, I tried but failed miserably to grasp what I was feeling.

It was such a feeling of disbelief. I felt a great sense of loss but a part of me refused to believe that he was actually gone. His clothes were still in my parents' bedroom, I could still smell his Old Spice cologne, I could still see his shoes in the closet. There was no way he could be gone, no way that he could leave me and leave me with my mom, who did not understand me the way he did. I don't even remember crying at that point, I just remember the heavy and unbearable burden of sadness.

Days later, I saw my mom wear a hat for the first time in my young life as we got into a car that took us to a church. I remember walking past many strangers, down what felt like the longest aisle I had ever seen, and my eyes fixed on the light grey casket that was at the front of the church. It was there that I would physically see my father for the very last time. I remember looking at his face and I could still see some of the injuries that he sustained. He just laid there, eyes tightly shut- tangible proof that he was really gone, in spite of my wild imaginations that this was just a horrible dream.

Thinking about it now, I know that the incredible sadness that I felt paled in comparison to what my mother must have felt. My uncle had one arm supporting her as she bit her lip through the tears that streamed down her face, while keeping his other arm around me. As I sat through the service, nothing made sense to me. I just remember laying my head down on someone's lap.

Next came the graveside service where we sat with roses ready to place on the casket as it went down into the ground. My father, my protector, my playmate, in spite of all of his challenges, was gone. As the crowds of visitors trickled to a stop, the reality of the events that transpired really started to set in. Loneliness became such a tangible reality.

My mother did not return to work for two months, she would simply cry. I remember begging to go back to school, I needed to get out of the house, back to some sense of normalcy until finally I was released to go back to my 2nd grade class.

My mom did her best to step into the role of being both parents, to raise me and my brothers, but she could never fill the gap that my father's death left. I know that it must have been horribly difficult for her to manage her emotions but as children, it was even more difficult for us to manage ours. I remember walking into a room one day and seeing my older brother curled up in the closet with a picture of our father in his arms as he cried his eyes out.

I do not think that our mother even considered that we would need some form of help to get us through this tragedy. I think she only realized how much pressure I was carrying on the inside when my hair began to fall out in large patches. Her response was to take me to a barber to cut my hair off. I don't have to tell you what that did to my self-esteem. I sunk even lower. I remember smiling through the pain, unable to articulate the brokenness that I felt. Those smiles would only continue to mask my pain in the years ahead. I did not know at that time that God was able to reach through the depths of my pain, and heal me. I am still learning, however, and I am grateful that I no longer have to hide behind a smile.

With my father gone, my mother began to find other ways to provide for her family. She had three children who all attended a private school and having moved into a new home, I am sure that she felt the burden of providing for her family as a single parent while still grieving her husband's death. As a passionate teacher, she looked for other opportunities and as a good teacher, she found many, including marking national exams as well as teaching night classes for students to have another opportunity to take national exams.

This undoubtedly helped not only to ease the financial burden of raising a family on her own but also to help her manage her emotions, or at least to help her cope by staying busy. She also hurled herself headlong into activities at her church. Over the next few years, she would do everything from drive the church bus to teach Sunday School, organize lunches and dinners, go to every service and do absolutely everything in between.

The thing is, no matter how hard or far we try to run, pain finds us when we do not take time to acknowledge it and submit it to God's healing power. As far as I know, my mother never dealt with her pain, she just kept herself busy and continued to be 'strong' in spite of everything going on.

As my mother submerged herself in a flurry of activities, I continued to struggle to make sense of the broken pieces of my little life. I had friends at school but of course none that I could talk to outside of hours because we were not allowed to use the telephone for long periods. Then things began to change in my family. I do not remember when it started but I would never forget some inappropriate touches that started from a close relative.

These touches would continue for years and would lead me down a dark path of masturbation and pornography. I would go through waves of shame and embarrassment and I got to the place that I would hear what I thought were my thoughts telling me that I was ugly, that I would never get married that my eyes were too big and a host of other lies, more than I can count. I had nowhere to turn, no one to talk to and many , many nights, I would just cry.

People would see a talented, funny and smart little girl who was so brave and 'strong'- at least on the outside. On the inside, I had no idea who I was but the little that I knew of me, was not who I wanted to be. I did not like the fact that I looked to moments of abuse to feel some form of 'affection' and attention.

The years became a blur until one summer when I was 11 that would change my life. I remember being at Vacation Bible School at my church and after a visiting group of young people came to work with us, I prayed the sinner's prayer for the first time. I surely did expect my life to change in that instant but it didn't as far as

I could tell, and for years to come, I would repeat that prayer so many times.

Looking back, I am so grateful for that first time that I said 'yes' because God planted a seed in me that grew and He patiently and lovingly covered me and protected me as I would make dumb decisions over and over in the years to come.

Chapter Three: Looking For Love In All The Wrong Places

When I completed eight grade, my mother decided that it would be cheaper to send me to another school. It was the first time I had attended a new school since first grade. I was thirteen and very aware of my sexuality and like any thirteen-year-old girl, I had a growing interest in boys. I was the new girl among students who had been to the same school since they were in kindergarten, and I did not know anyone. To make matters worse, the school that I came from was considered by this school to be 'snobbish' and I was labeled accordingly.

Loneliness was once again trying to take center stage in my life, until I met him...a handsome young man in the tenth grade who took the time to get to know me. He became my first 'real' boyfriend, and the person that I would give my virginity to. For the first time in a very long time, I felt 'loved'.

I have to pause here to say that it is absolutely essential to have someone in the lives of our children who can help to shift the narrative that the enemy is constantly playing in their heads and parents really should be to the forefront of this effort.

So back to this young man, he was very different from anyone that I had ever met, and at the tender age of thirteen, I gave away one of the most precious things that I could at that time, my virginity. For me, this was a very serious commitment, and I would spend the next few years of my life lying to my mother to spend every Saturday with him.

This was a significant turning point in my life, my innocence, whatever was left of it, was gone forever. This would also lead me down a very dark path, a path that I initially thought would lead me not only to true love but acceptance and peace. I would learn later that what I was looking for could only be found in Jesus.

I left the school that I began only a year earlier to return to my old school, I was back in familiar territory and back to old friends. I do not remember the exact moment that it happened but I ran into an old friend from a church trip, and I became fascinated with him. He was older and more mature and I began to spend time at his house after school. I was sixteen and he was nineteen.

I was still with my first real boyfriend at the time, but I began to spend more and more time with this young man. I would find out later on that he had just as much issues as I did, he was the black sheep of the family, the son of a preacher and taken in by an uncle because his parents lived in another country.

My attention soon began to drift away from my first boyfriend. Crazy enough I adopted this really dumb excuse for 'cheating' to justify my behavior. I would tell myself that every car needed a spare tire. The truth is, as I realize now, my self-esteem was still very low, I craved attention and what felt like love, and I was not secure in my identity. If I had only known my worth, I would not have wasted years of my life looking for validation and acceptance from other people, most of whom in the end were just as broken as I was. I would later learn that according to Ephesians 6:1, I was already accepted by God, and this acceptance had nothing to do with anything that I could ever have done, it is simply because of who He is.

Almost a year into my new relationship, my old boyfriend found out about my new boyfriend and he decided to leave.

I was absolutely fine with that because I was focused on my new boyfriend who I eventually became intimate with. Life was good, so I thought. I graduated from high school at sixteen and continued to see this young man. I eventually let my family know that I was seeing him.

At the age of 18, and I can remember exactly when it happened, I got pregnant. My heart sank when I found out the news, especially because I attended church every Sunday and my mom was very much involved with our church. I knew that she would have been disappointed, but I was slowly starting to wrap my head around what was happening.

I remember sitting on a couch that I sat in very often in the apartment that my boyfriend shared with his uncle and discussing the situation. He cried and cried and told me that he wasn't ready to have a child. He asked me to get an abortion because he just could not deal with having a child. In my mind, I really loved him and I would have done anything for him, so I decided that I would go through with the abortion. I have to pause here and say that in spite of what is being promoted in the times that we live in, an abortion is not the answer to an unwanted pregnancy.

The process to get to the hospital was a blur, I don't remember all of the details, but I do remember being so sad about all that was happening to me. I remember just crying- I was not ready to be a mother but I definitely was not prepared to go through this procedure. I remember laying on this table in an operating room in the hospital and the nurse made a comment to me about my boyfriend as I was given anesthesia and then blackness- no dreams, no thoughts. I woke up, what felt like hours later, in a hospital bed, feeling sore and incredibly empty- not just a physical emptiness but it felt like an emptiness in my soul.

This was a door that allowed me to escape from the weight of the consequences of my decision to have unprotected sex, but it did not take away the emotional damage that plagued me for years afterward. Looking back on it, I released that I was so happy to be 'loved' by this man, that I was willing to do anything to keep his 'love'. I also realize that my desire to be 'accepted' made me willing to cross just about any boundary. In reality we were both being quite irresponsible and selfish.

My self-esteem also hit another low, if that was possible. I found myself sinking to the point that even when this young man, who I thought I loved, began to emotionally abuse me, I stuck around because I didn't think that I could do any better. The thing about rejection is that it has many manifestations- I will address this in detail later, however, one of the things that I did was become more promiscuous.

Even while in this relationship, I continued to search for some level of validation from other men. Rejection is never satisfied. I eventually met another young man, very handsome and interesting. I never thought that someone like him would fall for me, so I was very caught up with him. Eventually I started sleeping with him, and once again I found myself pregnant. This time was very different- I was not in-love with him, I knew that I was just caught up with his looks. I was also still officially seeing my boyfriend and this young man had a girlfriend who was living in the United States at the time. I have to mention here that he and I were both involved in our local churches.

When I told him that I was pregnant, he immediately concluded that we needed to get married. I was surprised because while I knew that we were fooling around, I did not expect for things to progress that quickly and I found myself in a place that I did not understand- I wasn't particularly happy about marrying him, even though I felt like I didn't mind, I just wanted to be with someone who loved me. So he had a plan, he would leave his girlfriend and we would get married. I was on the bandwagon and things were looking up-at least on the outside. By this time I was around 19 and still not quite understanding the extent of this commitment that was being discussed.

While I still did not reconcile in my mind how I would begin to explain to my boyfriend that I was pregnant by someone else and about to marry that person, I still decided to move forward with the plan as discussed. I waited for my 'soon to be husband' to explain to his girlfriend that he could not be with her anymore.

When he came back to me after his conversation, however, things changed in an instant. When he went to speak with his girlfriend, he came back resolved that they would not break up and we needed to talk about how we would manage the child.

Rejected again-but I was not hurt, I was angry. How could he do this to me? I don't remember if he suggested that I get an abortion or if I decided to- the door was already opened and this time it was easier. Back to the hospital, back through the process but this time I was so angry that I was awake from surgery within an hour. I remember going by my best friend's house and talking with her. I remember the young man calling me or at least trying to, and I refused his calls. As a matter of fact, I refused to speak to him. I didn't feel the emptiness this time- I felt anger.

I really should have felt some level of remorse, but my hardened heart would not allow me to feel anything other than anger toward the young man, anger at myself for allowing myself to get caught in this situation again and more rejection.

Throughout my teenage years and early twenties I just tried everything that I could to run into relationships or just flings just to experience the focus of someone, if only temporarily. The truth is, we all have a void in our hearts that only God can fill. We can't fill it with sex, drugs, alcohol, medication, work or anything else but God. I did not know this at the time, so I just kept trying.

I stayed in the relationship with my second boyfriend, for a total of four years. Our relationship gradually became even more emotionally abusive and just unhealthy all around. I would stick around because I felt like I could not move forward without him because, the 'soul tie' between us was so strong.

The Bible does not lie, sexual intimacy is not designed to be experienced outside of the marital bed because it is more than a joining of bodies, it is also a joining at the spiritual, emotional and soul levels. Consistent sexual relationships and even casual ones connect us to the person whom we are intimate with. Have you ever noticed that couples who stay together for a long time can often finish each other's sentences or even anticipate what their partner would do or say? They become one. Soul-ties are a very important concept and for true healing and wholeness to take place, illegal soul ties have to be addressed. We will discuss in more detail in a later chapter.

So back to this boyfriend. I used to wear an anklet for a very long-time. It made me feel feminine and I'm sure that it also garnered attention, something that I longed for. I remember one night my boyfriend and I had an argument and he reached down and popped my gold anklet from my ankle. I was so angry that this became one of the first times I really asserted myself with him and stood up to him.

To show my defiance I went and bought a bigger one and almost dared him to touch it. In a lot of ways that was the beginning of the end- I was done. I started to see a young man at my work but again, this did not work out, he too began to use me- this time not only for sex but for my money. In spite of this, I found myself still going back to my second boyfriend, so finally I decided that I need to get away from him and everyone else, so I started looking for jobs on another island.

Finally, after weeks of applications, I got the job that I was looking for and with that, I prepared to leave, I just needed to get away, start fresh and begin to 'live'. By this time I was twenty years old. I recall my now ex-boyfriend still reaching out to me just to verbally remind me of how little he thought of me, and I clearly remember one night he called me a very unflattering word, to put it mildly. It was a curse word, and ordinarily I would have just mulled over what he had said, but this time was different and the reaction was almost instantaneous- I told him that his mother was actually what he was telling me that I was. He was so upset, and asked me how I could say that about his mother, when in fact it was him who introduced the word to the conversation. I hung up the phone and did not look back.

I moved to the other island and maintained very little contact with him. That is, until he decided to visit the island that I moved to. Coincidentally, or perhaps not, my best friend at the time decided to visit me around the same time.

I recall going to the airport to get my best friend and going to a part of the airport that I could see the passengers disembark. I was so happy to see her, it had been a while. I looked out of the large window and saw my best friend walking toward the terminal, but I also saw my ex-boyfriend, and to my absolute shock, they were holding hands. Imagine my hurt and disappointment, she was like a sister to me, and he was the person that I had spent four years of my life with. This was another level of betrayal and another blow of rejection for me.

Hurt people really do hurt people, and I did my best to hurt both of them in exchange for how they hurt me. While I indeed hurt them, the truth is I hurt myself in the process and I continued to experience hurt until I decided to forgive. My life was going in painful circles and cycles, looking for love and ending up disappointed each time.

After eight months, I decided to return home. By this time I had turned twenty-one. I continued to be promiscuous and continued cycles of destruction until my mom came to visit and began to introduce the concept of me returning home. Both of my brothers by now were married and only my nephew lived at home with my mom. I was convinced that I should come home only after my mother promised not to disrupt my independence. I had my plans, but God had His.

After returning home I met someone after going out late one night to a club. He was interesting, and definitely not the typical person that I would have gotten involved with. He was very assertive and commanded attention and I was so accustomed, by now, to having my own way, I was attracted to him.

As we spent more and more time together I started to consider for the first time that I wanted to get married, and I wanted to marry him. He felt the same way, or so I thought, and we went ahead and started discussing purchasing a property and the option of living behind his parents.' home The longer I spent with him though, the more I felt myself slipping away.

I did anything that he wanted me to do, I disconnected from friends, I began dressing in unflattering clothing, quite the opposite of the way that I used to dress. I would wear long skirts that stopped at my ankles and I pretty much allowed him to dictate to me in every aspect, with the exception of my anklet, I drew the line there.

I became more and more isolated from everyone, he was becoming my world, my 'god' and one thing I know for sure, God does not share. I was, of course, intimate with him, and quite careless with it, and this time, I found myself once again pregnant. This time, I was not willing to go down the road of having an abortion again. I was old enough to manage my own affairs, I had a job, we both did, and I was prepared to go through the embarrassment of being unwed and pregnant. My boyfriend, though, had different feelings. He had already had two other children and he did not want a third. With that I was once again in this all too familiar place.

THE TRUTH ABOUT ME

I remember going to the doctor's office, not quite sure what to say, but he had clearly seen the look on my face so many times in other patients that it was almost as if he read my mind. He asked me if I wanted an abortion and I told him that I did and right in his clinic he performed the procedure.

It was very different this time, it was so painful. It felt like whatever attempt at a painkiller he gave me only scratched the surface. I don't even remember how I got home but I do remember the feelings of emptiness, guilt and shame once again. I dealt with the physical pain but the emotional pain was only numbed by the fact that my boyfriend stayed with me.

One day, I was expecting him to come over and while I was waiting for him, I ended up in a conversation with a friend of mine and for some reason I ended up telling her about a man that I was intimate with when I was living on the other island. As I was telling her about what happened, my boyfriend came by but he just stood outside listening to my conversation. It was only afterward that he came inside.

I knew that something was wrong, but he kept saying that he was ok. We were intimate for the last time that night and afterward he called me back to tell me that it was over. He was upset about my conversation with my friend, even though I told him that this was an encounter that I had before I met him. I was devastated, he was the first person that I met that I never cheated on, and that I actually wanted to marry. I was broken...again.

Throughout all of this time, my mom remained emotionally unavailable, caught up in her own world and totally oblivious to what was happening with and to me. There were times that I blamed her for not being a better parent. I now realize though, that she gave me all that she could, but in her broken state, she just didn't have what I needed.

I remember, over the years writing faithfully in my diary about everything that I faced and even now I can look back with gratitude that God allowed me to have an outlet to express my wide range of emotions. My mom too was hurt, a victim of life's circumstances, and unfortunately, she never was healed and she suffered as a result. This is why we need to take the journey to heal, it is not just for us, but also for our children.

Chapter Four: The Dark Path of Pornography

I was a young girl, already familiar with inappropriate touching, from a young relative, and masturbation. The touching progressed to no longer being touched but instead to watching pornography with my abuser, who was also a child. So while the touching stopped, there was something left behind that dragged on for years into my future- an addiction to pornography and masturbation.

Some people erroneously think that watching pornography does not hurt anyone, but this could not be further from the truth. Sexual intimacy was designed by God Himself to be enjoyed between a husband and a wife. It is more than physical pleasure, it is a spiritual covenant and a very serious one at that. It is designed to be an integral part of this covenant relationship.

Sexual intercourse is a mystery, and the mystery is around the joining of the flesh also becoming a joining in the spirit and soul .As I wrote, Holy Spirit revealed something very profound- sexual intercourse is the only act that joins the 'entire man'. As human beings, we are triune beings- body, soul and spirit. Sexual intercourse connects two people on every level- the physical level, the spirit level and at the level of the soul. This is one of the reasons why the distortion of God's intended purpose and assignment for sexual intimacy is so dangerous. Anything that means something to God, becomes a key target area for the enemy because of his assignment which is to kill, steal and destroy (John 10:10), and nothing means more to God than us, His human creation. John 3:16 confirms this.

During the months that I started writing this book I had started listening to a number of testimonies from Missiondelafe.org[1], a wonderful non-profit organization that was started during the Covid-19 pandemic and is a platform for people who experienced and encountered Jesus. As I listened to some of the testimonies, I noted that quite a few of the people sharing their testimonies were introduced to pornography, and often at an early age, and it really made me think about how intentional the enemy is about distorting views about sexuality from an early age.

1 Corinthians 6:13 says *"You say, "Food for the stomach and the stomach for food, and God will destroy them both." The body, however is not meant for sexual immorality but for the Lord, and the Lord for the body."* New International Version.

Pornography shows a deviant view of sex, a view that not only glorifies fornication, which is sex outside of marriage, but also adultery, masturbation, homosexuality and every kind of deviant sexual behavior imaginable. It is a celebration of the flesh and everything that God does not want us to do. It is also highly spiritual and a very effective tool that Satan uses to entrap people. Additionally, it open doors to other addictions and other ways to destroy our bodies.

1 Corinthians 6:18-20 is very clear on God's position as it relates to sexual immorality. It says: *"[18]Flee from sexual immorality. All other sins a person commits are outside the body, but whoever sins sexually, sins against their own body. [19]Do you not know that your bodies are temples of the Holy Spirit, who is in you, whom you have received from God? You are not your own; [20]you were bought at a price. Therefore honor God with your bodies."* -New International Version.

Jesus paid a significant price for us, our freedom cost Him His very life! Knowing this, we must not be casual with how we treat our bodies and we must use our bodes to honor God.

For years, even after I got married, I struggled with pornography and masturbation, and like every other addiction, it was something that I thought I had under control without intervention. Speaking with and reading about people with addictions, I realize that there is a common deception, most people are fooled to thinking that they could stop at any time if they wanted to. This is not true, intervention is needed.

While the occasions became less and less frequent, even after I made up my mind to serve Jesus, I still struggled. I loved Jesus-yes, I surrendered my life to Him, I was serving Him, but I still struggled and I remember crying out to God many times afterward in repentance. I could not understand why it was so difficult.

I would watch pornography and masturbate, even though I had a healthy sex life and just cry out to God in shame afterward. I remember that there were two Scriptures that I would run to: *"Come now, and let us reason together, saith the LORD: though your sins be as scarlet, they shall be as white as snow; though they be red like crimson, they shall be as wool."* Isaiah 1:18 and Isaiah 59:1 *"Behold, the LORD's hand is not shortened, that it cannot save; neither his ear heavy, that it cannot hear"*

Even in my shame and guilt, God was reminding me that there was nothing that I could do that He could not cleanse me from, and that I could never move so far away from Him, that His Hand could not save me! I cried out to the Lord continuously and one day He stepped in and answered me, and completely removed the desires- cold turkey! He delivered me and I asked Him to remove the memories of what I watched, I renounced pornography and masturbation and I repented deeply, asked the Lord to forgive me and He truly did. It has been more than seventeen years now since He delivered me and to say that I am grateful is an understatement!

I want to pause to encourage you, there is nothing that you can possibly do that will cause God to love you any less or more than He does already. His love is not conditional, in fact He is love and because of His character, He loves and He loves deeply. The fact that He was willing to sacrifice His only Son, while we were still in our sinful states, is proof of the depth of His love for us. The enemy wants us to live lives of shame and defeat but God wants us to have abundant life!

This aspect of my journey has taught me a few things that I want to share with you. I will classify them into three categories- shame, guilt and condemnation, and freedom.

Shame

Merriam Webster dictionary defines shame as "a painful emotion caused by consciousness of guilt, shortcoming, or impropriety." Dictionary.com defines shame as "the painful feeling arising from the consciousness of something dishonorable, improper, ridiculous, etc., done by oneself or another." Both definitions have common themes- painful emotions connected to the awareness that a person has done something that they should not have done.

While I am no expert, I can say that based on my personal observations and readings, it appears that persons who are bound by addictions always battle with shame- the embarrassment of being connected to whatever it is that they are addicted to. What will people say or think? This alone can keep people in a perpetual state of unhappiness and shame.

Shame is a preferred tool of the enemy, primarily because it is self-inflicted. It is not based on the actual opinions of people, but based on your own opinion of yourself and a perceived opinion of others. Shame is a cage that ensnares many. It reminds me of the invisible fence concept. It is a psychological cage that keeps people bound until God intervenes. Pornography is tied to shame, and not just shame, a lot of other spirits, all with the same mission and that is to kill, steal from, and bring destruction to the person who is struggling.

Hebrews 12:1-2 says: *"1Therefore we also, since we are surrounded by so great a cloud of witnesses, let us lay aside every weight, and the sin which so easily ensnares us, and let us run with endurance the race that is set before us, 2looking unto Jesus, the author and finisher of our faith, who for the joy that was set before Him endured the cross,* ***despising the shame****, and has sat down at the right hand of the throne of God."* New King James Version, emphasis added.

This verse tells me that Jesus was quite acquainted with shame, however, He despised it. According to Merriam Webster Dictionary, despise means to look down on with disrespect or to regard as negligible, worthless, or distasteful. Jesus did not even consider shame worthwhile as He endured the cross because of what He desired to accomplish. He was beaten, slapped, spat on, whipped, stripped and forced to carry a cross to the most shameful and cursed public death, and in all of that He did consider the shame because He was so focused on His assignment. Shame was disregarded. These verses also tell us that Jesus is our example. Shame does not need to get the time of day from us because it is not as big an issue as the enemy would have us to feel. His plan is to keep us in the cycle of shame so that we would not think that freedom is possible.

Shame is actually tied to fear, the fear of people's opinions about something that we have done and the fear of what people may think of us as a result. The truth is there was only one perfect Man who ever walked this earth. Everyone else has or has had some issue, and in truth, something to be ashamed of. I am very surprised at the number of people who struggle with shame. If we allow it, shame can keep us quite bound because we can never heal from something unless we expose it and if we never expose it, then it stays unhealed. This is a demonic cycle of bondage.

When we expose what the enemy wants to keep us bound to, he can no longer work with the tool of shame. Practically, this looks like confessing or speaking about what we are ashamed of, and allowing God to shine His light on the place of pain and shame. This may be to God, a therapist, or a friend or trusted person who God directs you to. James 5:16 says: *"Confess your faults one to another, and pray one for another, that ye may be healed. The effectual fervent prayer of a righteous man availeth much."* King James Version. I do not think that the point here can be made any clearer.

When Jesus delivered me, He delivered me from the weight of my shame, but I held onto it for years after. He set me free, but I held on to the residue of my sin, until the Lord started to work in me to release my story, bit by bit. I had to learn that what I did was not a reflection of who I was. I may have been born into sin, but Jesus came so that I could be born again. My identity, who I am, has everything to do with who He created me to be and who I am in Him. I no longer have to carry around shame- as uncomfortable as I was about speaking about my past, the enemy can no longer use this against me because it has been exposed to the light of God's truth.

While I am ordinarily very private about certain aspects of my life, God clearly wanted me to expose these areas of my life because there are many still bound by the weight of shame and He wants you to know that you can be free- I am living proof, and there are many, many others who have experienced His freedom in this area, and you can also be added to this number.

I would like to close this point by saying you are not what you did. Shame attacks your self-esteem and your identity. Release it today and let God reveal who you really are.

Guilt and Condemnation
Guilt can be defined as ' feelings of deserving blame especially

for imagined offenses or from a sense of inadequacy'[2]. Condemnation can be defined as 'being pronounced guilty and sentenced to punishment'.[3] Guilt and condemnation are very closely related and they work in tandem. Sin in general is tied to guilt and condemnation. These spirits keep a person in a psychological space where they feel like they do not deserve good things, or freedom.

Pornography and masturbation leave a person not only feeling ashamed but also feeling guilty and condemned. Again these are primarily based on how the individual feels about themselves, not on what others think or on what a person actually deserves.

I have felt the burden of guilt and condemnation and again these are tools that the enemy loves to use so that we do not feel like we deserve freedom. Jesus gave His life long before we existed and extended the invitation for freedom, even while we were bound. Romans 5:8 in the New King James Version says *"But God demonstrates His own love toward us, in that while we were still sinners, Christ died for us."* God loved us before we ever knew ourselves, He is not moved by our sin, it does not scare Him, and it certainly does not shock Him. In fact, let's take a look at what God says in His Word in Psalms 103:

"1Bless the Lord, O my soul; And all that is within me, bless His holy name! 2Bless the Lord, O my soul, And forget not all His benefits: 3Who forgives all your iniquities, Who heals all your diseases, 4Who redeems your life from destruction, Who crowns you with lovingkindness and tender mercies, 5Who satisfies your mouth with good things, So that your youth is renewed like the eagle's. 6The Lord executes righteousness And justice for all who are oppressed. 7He made known His ways to Moses, His acts to the children of Israel. 8The Lord is merciful and gracious, Slow to anger, and abounding in mercy. 9He will not always strive with us, Nor will He keep His anger forever. 10He has not dealt with us according to our sins, Nor punished us according to our iniquities.

11*For as the heavens are high above the earth, So great is His mercy toward those who fear Him;*
12*As far as the east is from the west, So far has He removed our transgressions from us."*

King David wrote this Psalm, and he was known for both his sin, and his willingness to always go to God and seek His forgiveness. He was also known as a worshipper, to the extent that God referred to him as a 'man after His own heart' (Acts 13:22). What I have learned about guilt is that is causes us to run away from God. Look at Adam in the book of Genesis after he had eaten the fruit that was forbidden by God, he hid.

The weight of guilt and condemnation could drive us in the opposite direction from God, but like little children, God wants us to run to Him, not from Him, even in these times. Think about it, nothing is hidden from Him anyway- He wants us to come, His arms are outstretched, He wants to purify us, to wash us and reward us with freedom. God not only abounds in mercy but He delights in mercy, according to Micah 7:18, and His mercy endures forever, according to Psalm 136.

One of the greatest revelations of worship that I have received is the fact that worship is an exchange. Sometimes worship is perceived as a song or words of adoration to God, and yes that can be a part of it, but worship is also bringing our issues, our challenges, our shame, our guilt and condemnation in exchange for His grace, mercy, peace and forgiveness. Every last one of our sins Jesus died for, there is no need to carry the weight of guilt. Isaiah 53:6 says *"All we like sheep have gone astray; We have turned, every one, to his own way; And the LORD has laid on Him the iniquity of us all."* King James Version

I have to pause and thank Jesus for carrying burdens that were too great for us to bear, and allowing us to experience freedom, even when we deserved punishment. I stumbled upon a verse the other day that even drove this point further home for me. Revelation

1:5-6 says: "and from Jesus Christ, who is the faithful witness, and the first begotten of the dead, and the prince of the kings of the earth. **Unto Him that loved us, and <u>washed us from our sins in His own blood</u>**, and hath made us kings and priests unto God and His Father; to Him be glory and dominion for ever and ever. Amen." King James Version- emphasis added. This is no ordinary love! To know that Jesus took my sin, and I mean ALL of them and to washed them in HIS OWN BLOOD-the result of His pain and sacrifice, is absolutely mind blowing!

Freedom

John 8: 31-38 says :"*31To the Jews who had believed him, Jesus said, "If you hold to my teaching, you are really my disciples.32Then you will know the truth, and the truth will set you free." 33They answered him, "We are Abraham's descendants and have never been slaves of anyone. How can you say that we shall be set free?" 34Jesus replied, "Very truly I tell you, everyone who sins is a slave to sin.35Now a slave has no permanent place in the family, but a son belongs to it forever.36So if the Son sets you free, you will be free indeed.*" New International Version

This Scripture says a whole lot about freedom. Jesus was in a conversation with the religious sects at that time and was imparting some very important principles that are summarized below:

- Jesus' disciples are not those who just follow Him, but those who hold to and obey His teachings. These teachings are rooted in God's Word. His Word is absolute truth and gives knowledge of the truth, and the truth brings freedom.

- The people who Jesus was speaking to objected to what He was saying because as far as they were concerned, they were never slaves and as a result, they did not need to be set free.

- Jesus, however, rebutted their objection by letting them know that anyone who sins is a slave to sin. Sin slaves do not have a place in God's family, only sons. When the Son of God sets us free, we are truly free.

My freedom came from God Himself! Because He has set me free, I am truly free! You may not have this struggle, you may struggle with something else- the principle, however, remains the same- Jesus can and will set us free if we allow Him to do so. The key is for us to let Him in and for us to understand that there is no sin that is greater than God's ability to deliver!

There are times that guilt, shame and condemnation can make us feel like we are beyond the redemption of God. The truth is that we are never beyond His redemption. In Psalms 139, the Psalmist went into detail about how deeply God knows us and the fact that there is nowhere that we can go from His presence.

Pornography and masturbation both please the flesh and the flesh opposes things of the Spirit of God. They are both rooted in pride- what I want, what I feel. Pride centers us around ourselves, making us 'gods' of our own lives. Pride puts us in opposition to God and God does not tolerate any other god and not only this, He fights against the proud.

Pride is one of the ways that the enemy keeps people in bondage because as long as we could be deceived into walking in pride, we will be far from God's grace. Proverbs 16:5 says: *"The LORD detests the proud; they will surely be punished."* New Living Translation. James 4:6 says: *"And he gives grace generously. As the Scriptures say, "God opposes the proud but gives grace to the humble."* New Living Translation.

It is important to note that even after God sets us free, we have to steward our freedom. This means being very intentional about not putting ourselves in a position to be entrapped again. Freedom does not mean that we will never experience temptation, but it does mean that once we continually submit ourselves to God, we are strengthened to resist the enemy and he has to leave, in accordance with James 4:7.

One of the reasons that this is so critical is that when we have experienced deliverance and we do not turn away from the sin that brought us to the place of bondage in the first place, we risk being in a worse position when we re-open the door to the enemy. In Luke 11:24-26 says: *"24 When an impure spirit comes out of a person, it goes through arid places seeking rest and does not find it. Then it says, 'I will return to the house I left.'25When it arrives, it finds the house swept clean and put in order.26Then it goes and takes seven other spirits more wicked than itself, and they go in and live there. And the final condition of that person is worse than the first."* New International Version. This verse shows us the danger in not stewarding our freedom.

Living a life of freedom requires consistent intentionality. While Jesus is the source of this freedom, there is a level of effort that we have to make in order to keep this freedom. Practically, this sometimes looks like walking away from friendships, or lovers, or habits, or even comfort zones. In my case, it looked like being very cautious about the things that I watched, and even around some conversations that promoted illicit sex or carnality.

I am very mindful, to this day, of what I allow before my eyes, pictures that I look at and even reading material. I had to guard my freedom and ask God to help me. Does it mean that I was never tempted? Not at all, but I continued to fight to keep my freedom by God's grace. There were times that the enemy would even attack me in my sleep though my dreams but I would always go to God when I awoke and ask Him to remove every demonic seed planted.

As you stand and guard your freedom, the day will come when the fight will become easier. God is so faithful, He will reward your faithfulness in standing strong in your freedom.

Chapter Five: Rejection

R ejection can start at any point, even in the womb. Everyone wants to be accepted and loved, even from they are babies, and I was no different. Unfortunately, while I did not have the language for it, I did experience rejection at an early age. In fact, as I started to put pieces together and God began to reveal some things to me, I began to understand how this spirit impacted my life.

I have no doubt that my father loved my mother, but he struggled with what I now know is a spirit of perversion. As a result, he was very promiscuous and he continued to see other women while he was married to my mother. When I was much older, my mother would tell me stories about some of the challenges that she faced in her marriage. There was one story that she told me that I never understood the fullness of until much later in life.

She told me that during that time that she had me, married women had to have their husbands sign paperwork in order to have their tubes tied, otherwise the doctor would not perform the procedure. My mother, had just given birth to me, and while still in the hospital, she asked a man who came in her hospital room to change the garbage bin, if he could read. When he confirmed that he could, my mother asked him to sign the paperwork, essentially pretending to be my father, in order for her to get her tubes tied. Armed with this forged signature, she gave this information to the doctor and he went ahead and performed the procedure. Just like that, she made sure that there would be no more children from their union.

While I can only speculate about the reasons that she took these drastic steps, I do understand that she must have been desperate to do what she did to ensure that she never found herself in this position again. I did experience love from my parents yet I also felt distance-there was an emotional disconnect. From an adult's perspective now, I can see that this distance may not have been intentional, they may have just been caught up in their own worlds. Unfortunately, this absence of attention for a child can be devastating. Children need to be nurtured and given lots of love and attention, especially in their earlier years.

I cannot pinpoint when I started to feel like I did not belong, but I recognize that the spirit of rejection definitely found its way to me and it was something that I had battled with for years up to fairly recently. The enemy is so strategic in trying to ensure that even from birth, some people experience rejection. While I am unable to say if rejection was an issue at birth, I can say that I felt it very early in my life and as I got older I felt it in different ways from different people, family and non-family and it played a significant role in the decisions that I made as I matured.

I can see how the enemy was quite intentional on presenting situations that took me deeper and deeper into cycles of rejection. I was rejected by my family and even when I got married, I experienced bouts of rejection and eventually I began to reject myself the way I did when I was a child.

Rejection is a demon spirit that manifests itself in many ways, too many to name at this moment, but I will expand on the ways that I have seen it manifest in my life. These ways are noted below:

Perfectionism

One would think that being a perfectionist is a good thing, but looking deeper, the root of it is not. Being a perfectionist often manifests like wanting things to be perfect so that people can be seen in a particular light. The truth is that we all have flaws and we all make mistakes. The fact that we are humans who came after the fall of Adam means that we have sin and therefore are imperfect. Jesus was the only perfect Man who ever walked the earth

In my life, I tried to get as close to perfect as possible so that people would not see my pain and shame and would instead see me as this perfect person, which in reality, I definitely was not. I focused on getting great grades, doing and saying the right things so that I would be liked or accepted.

I must pause here to say that there is a difference between being a perfectionist and operating with an excellent spirit. In Daniel 6:3, the Bible says that Daniel was preferred above the princes and presidents because he had an excellent spirit within Him. The primary difference here is that a perfectionist's actions are all self-driven and with a singular motive that self is promoted. When a person has an excellent spirit it is excellence driven by the Lord and He alone gets the glory from it, not the person.

I used to think being a perfectionist is a good thing, until I understood its connection to the spirit of rejection. Motives matter to God and anything that promotes self over Him is not a good thing, regardless of the end result. The thing is, there is a clear distinction in what we do and who we are- doing things do not change who we are as people. When we give our lives to God in submission, all that we are is rooted in Him. Our only pursuit should be to please Him and what pleases Him is our heart's posture toward Him, not the things that we can do.

People Pleasing

This happens when people seek 'acceptance' by doing things that would please other people, not because there is a pure motive of genuinely wanting the person to be happy but from a motive of wanting the person to see them in a more favorable light and therefore 'accept' them. This practice could actually be very dangerous because sometimes we do things that harm ourselves or put us in uncomfortable positions simply to be accepted. This can also look like peer pressure where people pressure others into doing or nor doing things. The reality is that some of the people that we work so hard to please do not always or even sometimes have our best interests at heart.

I cannot even say how many times I did things that I was not comfortable doing, just because I wanted someone to think that I was 'cool' or a team player or I because I was afraid that the person would think different of me or would dislike me if I did not do what I did. In truth, if a person only likes us because of what we can do for them, then this is not the type of relationship that we want or need. Meaningful and productive friendships are those rooted in unconditional love and acceptance, not based on what can be gained by one side.

People pleasing for me also looked like not wanting to say how I really felt about a situation or simply avoiding uncomfortable discussions, again because I did not want to be viewed in a particular light. Looking back at this now, I can see that in this instance, the spirit of rejection partnered with the spirit of intimidation and fear so that I would be more consumed by what someone thought of me than being consumed by speaking up and speaking truth. In some circumstances, when we do not say something, people may get hurt or the individual may be disadvantaged, because they may repeat cycles of behavior that are not acceptable, and by not saying something it may leave them with the false impression that the behavior is, in fact, acceptable.

I also realized just how selfish this type of behavior really is. When we love others, we speak truth to them, and when we love ourselves we set boundaries. Speaking truth is a form of correction. Proverbs 3:12 says: *"For the LORD corrects those he loves, just as a father corrects a child in whom he delights."* New Living Translation. Because we love, we correct, even as the perfect example that God has given us.

I can see why the enemy uses this manifestation of rejection, because so many of these manifestations can take us deeper and deeper into bondage if we do not shift from these behaviors.

Insecurity and Feelings of Inferiority

These emotions lead a person to feel like they are not good enough to be accepted or even that they are not valuable in the sight of others. These emotions also make a person feel like they do not 'fit in'. Even though some persons pretend like they do not need others, the truth is we were created for community. We need each other and we need to feel accepted. The older I grew, the more I felt like I did not fit in and this often led to some very destructive behavior.

From very early in life, I did not see myself as beautiful or someone of worth and because of this I almost idolized anyone who, at least in my mind, did. Allowing thoughts of inferiority opened doors to depression and even consideration of suicide, especially when I was younger. These emotions are devices used by the enemy to attempt to devalue us and diminish the truth about who we are.

God loved us enough to sacrifice His only Son so that He could redeem us back to Himself. He thought we were worth it, He thought we were worth this great price. When we partner and begin to agree with the emotions of insecurity and inferiority, it is contrary to what God thinks and it is actually a manifestation of pride. Be reminded that pride is making oneself god of their own life. When we think that we are 'less than' we are saying 'God we disregard what You think and what we think is not only better, but it is truth', when in fact it could not be further from the truth!

Psalms 139:14 says *"I will praise You, for I am fearfully and wonderfully made; Marvelous are Your works, And that my soul knows very well."* New King James Version. God took His time to make us, He spoke everything else into existence but took time to form us with His hands, in His image and likeness (Genesis 1:27).

I have come to realize that our viewpoint of ourselves is very far from God's viewpoint. He sees His image and likeness when He looks at us, I'm sure that it hurts Him to see how we sometimes diminish and devalue ourselves.

I spent years being uncomfortable in my own skin, but bit by bit, this viewpoint transformed and I know it is because of God healing my erroneous viewpoints and exposing the lies from the enemy that I believed. Say these words with me: I AM LOVED, I AM ACCEPTED, I AM WORTH IT!

Gossiping

While this may not seem like an obvious manifestation of the spirit of rejection, it is. I always loved to talk, to be seen and heard, of course because I wanted people to like me and to see me or at least a palatable version of me. Talking about others gave me a sense that others were in a worse position than I was and it was a way of deflecting my issues so that people would not see me but see the person that I was talking about, and as a result, think more highly of me.

Gossip is hurtful, to say the least and it is something that God detests and He has quite a bit to say about gossiping or talebearing in His word. Below are just a few Scriptures that speak to this spirit, I would encourage you to research others, if this is something that you struggle with.

1. A perverse man sows strife, And a whisperer separates the best of friends.- Proverbs 16:28 (NKJV)

2. He who goes about as a talebearer reveals secrets; Therefore do not associate with one who flatters with his lips.- Proverbs 20:19 (NKJV)

3. Let no corrupt word proceed out of your mouth, but what is good for necessary edification, that it may impart grace to the hearers.- Ephesians 4:29 (NKJV)

4. Where there is no wood, the fire goes out; And where there is no talebearer, strife ceases. - Proverbs 26:20 (NKJV)

5. But shun profane and idle babblings, for they will increase to more ungodliness.- II Timothy 2:16 (NKJV)

6. A talebearer reveals secrets, But he who is of a faithful spirit conceals a matter.- Proverbs 11:13 (NKJV)

7. Let all bitterness, wrath, anger, clamor, and evil speaking be put away from you, with all malice.- Ephesians 4:31 (NKJV)

While the Scriptures all give a very good indication of God's feelings, I would like to comment briefly on the third mentioned verse. When we know The Lord, our words are supposed to uplift and edify people, not destroy. It does not mean that we are not to speak truth, but it is important to speak truth in love according to Ephesians 4:15. I observed that when we speak truthfully with a motive of love there is healing and even though it may be hard to hear the truth, the backing of love makes it more palatable and helps the person to see the value in what is being said so that they can make the necessary changes.

I would be remiss if I did not mention the following scripture, which is an excellent indication of God's feelings about sowing discord:

"16These six things the Lord hates, Yes, seven are an abomination to Him: 17A proud look, A lying tongue, Hands that shed innocent blood, 18A heart that devises wicked plans, Feet that are swift in running to evil, 19A false witness who speaks lies,

And one who sows discord among brethren." -Proverbs 6: 16-19 King James Version- Emphasis added

Gossipping sous discord among brothers. Bibleref.com puts it this way:

"The ESV (English Standard Version) translates this sin as those who "sow discord." To "sow" is a reference to farming and means to deliberately plant seeds. The person who "sows discord" uses gossip, lies, unfounded accusations, negative criticism, and backbiting to accomplish his goal. The result which "sprouts" from those actions is strife. Life is hard enough, as it is—it's deeply sinful to create even more conflict between those who ought to be working together."

This is such a profound statement. God, who is love, hates when people cause division by sowing seeds of discord. This is a very serious, serious matter.

Rejection in any manifestation is extremely destructive, and at the heart of it is pride. Ephesians 1:3-6 says: "*3Blessed be the God and Father of our Lord Jesus Christ, who has blessed us with every spiritual blessing in the heavenly places in Christ, 4just as He chose us in Him before the foundation of the world, that we should be holy and without blame before Him in love, 5having predestined us to adoption as sons by Jesus Christ to Himself, according to the good pleasure of His will, 6to the praise of the glory of His grace, by which He made us accepted in the Beloved.*"- New King James version- Emphasis added.

God chose us before He created the world and we were predestinated or determined before -hand to be adopted as His sons and daughters, we are chosen- in spite of our inadequacies and failures, chosen by the Almighty God to be His children, adopted into His family!!!

We may reject ourselves, people may reject us, but God accepted us, and His opinion and truth trumps any other opinion or truth, including our own! The God who created the heavens and the earth has accepted us, and as a result there is no place that rejection belongs in our lives.

While this is something that I really wish I learned earlier in life, I am so glad that I am fully aware of it now. God has delivered me from the spirit of rejection, my aim is to please Him in everything that I do and this means that I have to love myself because He has shown me my value and worth and I understand the lengths that He went to in order to rescue me. I am worth it because He demonstrated that I am.

My prayer is that God opens your eyes to see just how much you are valued and the extent to which He went to draw you to Himself. He loves you, He has chosen you, He has redeemed you through His Son, and He has accepted you!

Chapter Six: Pain, Pain and More Pain

As much as we would like to avoid pain, it is impossible. Inevitably we will all experience pain in some form between the time that we enter the earth and leave the earth. Pain can be physical, psychological and emotional, and like you, I experienced pain, perhaps in more ways than I expected. The thing about pain though, is you can learn from it, you can grow from it, and you can definitely heal from it, not in your strength alone, but with God's help.

One of the most painful experiences that I had early in my life was the pain of losing my father. He was definitely not an angel and not a saint by any stretch of the imagination, but he was my dad and I loved him. Even in my adulthood I found out some things about him that have opened my eyes to who he was, but even in this and based on my knowledge at this stage in my life, I know that he too experienced levels of pain and while he obviously cannot say, his actions told me that he never dealt with his pain, his trauma or hurt. If he did, his life would have been very different from the way it was.

There is a very true saying- 'hurt people hurt people' and this is something that I lived and continue to observe even now.

Throughout my childhood and well in to adulthood, I experienced the pain of loneliness. I would literally be in a room full of people and still feel alone and that no one understood me. I remember one day, just a few years ago, a friend of mine who is a prophetess ministered to me and God gave her a glimpse of the pain that I carried around for so long, I didn't even realize that I was carrying it- because I had grown numb to it. God came after loneliness that day and He reminded me that He is my Daddy. I cried and cried and cried that day, because for so long, I thought that I was alone, I believed the lie. That day I knew that He saw me, I could have related to Hagar when God told her that He saw her- He is truly the God who sees.

Even as I grew older and I began to get into romantic relationships, I experienced pain, in particular the pain of heartbreak. When I dated the last person before I met my husband, I really felt like this was the 'one' for me, the person who would be my husband and love me forever- only to find out that he was not. I was so hurt, I almost could not function. I did not want to eat, could not sleep, I could not function at work, I was a hot mess- to say the least. My manager pulled me aside one day and told me to get it together. While this made me realize just how much this pain had immobilized me, even though I started to do my work, it was incredibly difficult for me to manage or function.

Above all of this, I was angry with God. This is absolutely absurd to me now as an older adult but I surely was upset with God, in spite of the fact that I never committed my relationship to Him or even asked Him if the relationship was what He wanted for me. I know that God must have laughed at my disposition toward Him, in His shoes I would have laughed too. I stopped praying, didn't want Him to say anything to me, I just wanted to be alone and not bothered by anyone including Him. I'm so glad that God, in His loving mercy, politely ignored my tantrum and still stepped in to rescue me from my destructive behavior. It was only when God shared a Scripture verse in a dream that I began to function. This was one of the first times I had experienced this type of encounter with God and it spoke directly to my hurt.

In my marriage I experienced pain and disappointment as well. I can think of many times when all I could do is cry and feel sorry for myself. I would function at work during the day, pay attention during my schooling at night and then come home to feel empty all over again. I think if I could add up all of the times that I cried, it would add up to years. I once heard Joyce Meyers speaking about sleeping on the seam of the mattress and I quite easily related to what she was referring to- not wanting to be near your spouse because of hurt and devastation.

From my vantage point now, I can see that both my husband and I were broken and in need of healing, and the pain that we lived with individually influenced us in our marriage and spilled over into our decisions and eventually on to our children. I have to pause here to say, please take the time to take the journey of healing, it is not just for you.- future generations and future relationships depend on it!

I feel like marital pain is a very different type of pain, especially when infidelity is involved. Many people daydream of getting married to the man or woman of their dreams and living happily ever after. I have yet to see a perfect marriage, and mine is no exception. I have experienced hurt to numbness and I cannot even begin to describe how excruciating this pain could be, there were times when I felt like my world was crumbling around me. In my culture infidelity is so prevalent and it is referred to as 'sweet-hearting' but the reality is that there is absolutely nothing sweet about this. This type of behavior destroys families- one act of 'pleasure' can lead to emotional trauma not only for the spouse but also for children in the marriage.

Infidelity is the epitome of selfishness- it is all about what I want, who I want to be with, and I don't care who gets hurt in the process. It has lasting effects on families and nothing good comes from it- it is simply another trap of the enemy to bring destruction to homes and the holy covenant of marriage.

Looking back over my life, I see many instances of pain, hurt and disappointment, but I can also see that whenever I placed my faith and hope in people and not God, I experienced pain that was almost too difficult to bear. I put people in the place where only God should have been and I paid dearly for it every time. Please do not misunderstand me, again, God created us to be a part of communities. The challenge, however, is when we begin to look up to people, as if they are our 'gods', when in fact they are simply human beings, just like us, complete with flaws and shortcomings.

There is also a level of disappointment and pain that can be based on misplaced confidence in ourselves as well, and in our inability to do things that we would like to be done. I also learned the hard way that I am not invincible and I do not have all of the answers, as a matter of fact, if left to my own devices, I would make self-destructive decisions on a more frequent basis than I would like to admit.

I often use the term –"But God", and it could not be more accurate to describe my life. If it had not been for God's intervention and His willingness to rescue me, even from myself, I would be long gone, I would be an absolute failure, I would be nowhere doing absolutely nothing.

His grace has sustained me, even through my dumb decisions, and my misplaced hope. He lovingly guided me and directed my steps and even allowed my missteps to be turned around to bring me closer to Him.

There is no pain that is unbearable when we are in God. He created our emotions and He understands how we feel, all of the time. He invites us to come to Him and bring our hurts and disappointments. Psalms 62:8 says: *"Trust in Him at all times, you people; Pour out your heart before Him; God is a refuge for us. Selah"* New King James Version. This was a key that I learned later in life but I am still grateful that I learnt it.

I believe that God wants me to share on pain because everyone experiences it at some point in their lives, and some people experience it more than others. In my life, my own pain affected my decisions in just about every aspect. People often see the 'finished product' and sometimes conclude that we have it all together. The reality is that in this journey called life, pain is a part of the process that shapes us and if we manage it carefully, or rather God's way, we can in fact make it to the other side of pain.

In my life, one may think that I always kept it together, but the truth is I was very good at hiding my pain behind smiles and jokes and at some point, even religion. Although I attempted to start the journey of healing through therapy and even personal coaching, God's instruction to me was to write this book. Through obedience to this instruction for me, I actually found myself being stripped of the layers that I hid behind for years. I am finding it easier to share about my experiences with abuse, and pornography addiction and even abortions. It is crazy how the more I share, the more I hear about people who would have experienced the exact same thing, and who are still struggling with shame and pain.

There is a path for healing from your pain too. It starts with a willingness to face yourself and a willingness to be vulnerable before God. He knows anyway, and He knows the root cause of it and He also knows how to heal you and set you free. When He reveals the path, it is important to obey.

I have to admit, as I stated in the introduction, I was not exactly thrilled about this journey, I am a private person and this book was NOT my choice as a means to go through healing. I delayed and dragged my feet and while I told God 'yes' with my lips, my heart and my actions said ' NO'. Finally, I gave in when God gave me a deadline to finish this book and I actually missed the first deadline, not because I said no again, I just got busy and distracted. I did ask Him for an extension and I promised both

Him and myself that I would not miss it.

Even as I started the earlier chapters and sat through my pain as I wrote, I started to see a difference in my perspective and outlook on life and the test came through friendships that were really dear to me. I lost some really good friends during the process of writing this book, and not through death.

Hearts were revealed to me and I saw ugly jealousy in one and another just walked away. In the past I would have been devastated at the losses, but I simply cried out to God and told Him about my hurt and disappointment, and He heard me and gave me a peace that I still cannot explain.

I was very careful to walk in forgiveness because I understand that God forgives me when I forgive others. Matthew 6: 14-15 says: "*14For if you forgive men their trespasses, your heavenly Father will also forgive you. 15But if you do not forgive men their trespasses, neither will your Father forgive your trespasses.*" New King James Version.

Also, it was important to forgive quickly so that I would not start to become bitter. Ephesians 4: 31-32 says: "*31Get rid of all bitterness, rage, anger, harsh words, and slander, as well as all types of evil behavior. 32Instead, be kind to each other, tenderhearted, forgiving one another, just as God through Christ has forgiven you.*" New Living Translation

Hebrews 12:15 says: "*looking carefully lest anyone fall short of the grace of God; lest any root of bitterness springing up cause trouble, and by this many become defiled;*" New King James Version

These Scriptures highlight the importance of ensuring that we do not become bitter. Sometimes pain can lead to bitterness and other emotions that, if left unchecked, can start to harden our hearts toward others and even toward God. When our hearts become hardened we no longer respond to Him and His desires and we head for certain destruction.

I have to go back to look at the term 'root of bitterness' mentioned in Hebrews 12:15. Merriam-Webster Dictionary has several definitions for the word 'root', however, two of them stood out to me:

1. "The usually underground part of a seed plant body that originates usually from the hypocotyl, functions as an organ of absorption, aeration and food storage or as a means of anchorage and support, and differs from a stem especially in lacking notes, buds and leaves;" and
2. "something that is an origin or source (as of a condition or quality).

Let's further break down a few terms using the Merriam-Webster dictionary:

- Absorb means to take something in
- Aeration/aerate means to supply or impregnate

The root is something that is usually under the surface. If there is a root of bitterness, it may not be evident to us or even those around us that we are bitter and that something is growing in the dark, soon to be revealed. It is the 'organ' that is responsible for taking in the nutrients, and supplying the plant as it grows. Roots also gain strength, the longer they grow. If we do not pluck up the root while it is tender, it will become more difficult to pull up, the longer it stays and becomes entrenched. To get a clear understanding of what God is saying let's take a look at the surrounding verses in Hebrews 12:

Hebrews 12:14 *"Pursue peace with all people, and holiness, without which no one will see the Lord: 15looking carefully lest anyone fall short of the grace of God; lest any root of bitterness springing up cause trouble, and by this many become defiled; 16lest there be any fornicator or profane person like Esau, who for one morsel of food sold his birthright. 17For you know that afterward, when he wanted to inherit the blessing, he was rejected, for he found no place for repentance, though he sought it diligently with tears"*

These verses start with pursuing peace as well as holiness. Pursuit is a very intentional act, there is nothing passive about it. We have to be intentional about the pursuit of peace with all people as well as holiness. The thing is, it does not mean that we will get along with everyone, but it does mean that we are deliberate about going after peace with people. Holiness also requires intentionality and I know that God Himself is quite intentional when it comes to His Word. Pursuing peace with all people and holiness are two actions grouped together and they are not unrelated. I believe that holiness is not the absence of sin, I believe that holiness is pleasing God. When we live to please God, a by-product would be obedience to His Word which tells us how to live. So if we pursue peace with people and holiness, we do not have to be concerned about bitterness developing roots.

These verses also speak about the fact that bitterness defiles or makes us unclean and takes us away from holiness. Once this happens, we end up doing and saying ungodly things as this root grows and establishes itself.

I wanted to spend some time on this because pain can lead to bitterness, which can lead to defilement and profane acts. Again considering these verses, especially when looking at Esau, there is an inference that he was influenced by bitterness and as a result, he ended up making a decision that cost him his inheritance. This tells me about the dangers of bitterness because as it established, it influences our decisions. Having a heart's desire to please God requires us to take time to make sure that our thoughts please Him, our words please Him and our actions please Him.

Pain is not something that we can avoid, but it is something that we can release to God and allow Him to heal us. There are quite a few Scriptures about God declaring His nearness to the broken and contrite heart. Before we look at them, let's look at the definitions for 'broken' and 'contrite'.

Broken[4] means violently separated into parts or shattered; damaged; having undergone or been subjected to fracture; made weak; crushed or sorrowful

Contrite[5] means feeling or sharing sorrow or remorse for improper or objectionable behavior or actions. Synonyms include the words "apologetic", "penitent", "regretful", "remorseful", "repentant" and "sorry".

The following verses are just a few Scriptures that speak to God's response to a heart that is broken and contrite.

Psalms 51:17 (NKJV)
The sacrifices of God are a broken spirit, A broken and a contrite heart — These, O God, You will not despise.

Psalms 34:18 (NKJV)
The Lord is near to those who have a broken heart, And saves such as have a contrite spirit.

Isaiah 57:15 (NKJV)
For thus says the High and Lofty One Who inhabits eternity, whose name is Holy: "I dwell in the high and holy place, With him who has a contrite and humble spirit, To revive the spirit of the humble, And to revive the heart of the contrite ones.

Isaiah 66:2 (NKJV)
For all those things My hand has made, And all those things exist," Says the Lord . "But on this one will I look: On him who is poor and of a contrite spirit, And who trembles at My word.

God will not ignore a heart that is broken before Him. Not just broken, but contrite or repentant- a heart that will turn away from what is not of Him, and turn to Him. As I stated before, David was known as a man after God's heart. He was no saint, by any stretch of the imagination, but his heart was broken and contrite before God. Whenever he sinned, he cried out to God and worshipped

Him, he never ran away from God, he always ran to Him with his brokenness.

It does not matter what we have done, when we bring our hearts to Him and offer Him our brokenness, God will step in and address the pain. I did not always know that I could run to Him. My issues and challenges caused me to run away from Him, like Adam after he had sinned, but I have come to learn that in our pain, in our shame, in our weakness God wants us to run, not away from Him, but to Him. There is nothing that we could do that could surprise Him or separate us from His love for us.

I absolutely love the way The Passion Translation positions Romans 8: 35: *"Who could ever divorce us from the endless love of God's Anointed One? Absolutely no one! For nothing in the universe has the power to diminish His love toward us. Troubles, pressures, and problems are unable to come between us and heaven's love. What about persecutions, deprivations, dangers, and death threats? No, for they are all impotent to hinder omnipotent love,"*

As I conclude this chapter, I encourage you to meditate on this verse. I am very much acquainted with pain, perhaps too much to write about, but God's love confronted my pain when I gave it to Him. Practically this looks like literally telling God about how we feel, and telling Him that we release these emotions and we give these feelings to Him, and resting in the knowledge that He loves us deeper than the pit that pain is trying to place us in.

God is not like man, He does not hold grudges, when He forgives, He forgets- according to His Word.

Chapter Seven: Identity

Have you ever had something really expensive like a diamond or a nice car or a very expensive piece of clothing or a watch? Or have you ever worked really hard to save and purchase something? In both cases, when you have something of exceptional value or worth, you would treat it different from your other possessions that are less expensive and less valuable because you understand its value and the sacrifices that you made to get it.

Now, imagine someone who has no idea of the history or value of this item, comes along and treats your valuable item casually or carelessly. You would be very upset, I know I would. The thing is, if they do not have an appreciation for the value of this item or what you had to do to get this valuable item, they would not treat it the same way you would.

God went through great lengths and made the ultimate sacrifice to redeem us to Himself. He sent His one and only Son to die so that we may live, yet we handle our own lives very casually because we do not understand our own worth and value. Many people do not understand exactly who they are and their own worth- I was one of them, and I am still learning.

I never knew that I did not understand who I was until one day when I was asked one seemingly 'simple' question – who are you? I could not answer right away, even after careful thought, I still could not answer this question. Even when I started to form a response in my head, the only things that came to mind was my name and the roles that I played like wife, mother and employee. This question puzzled me for a bit because at that time I was in my early forties and I was baffled at how such a simple question could have me so stumped.

If I had known my true identity, I would not have handled my own life so casually, I would have made many different decisions because I would have understood my value. I am writing this chapter so that if you do not know who you are and your value, you would gain a better understanding of your precious worth.

We were created to please God, we were created to become His sons and daughters- sons and daughters of the King of kings. There are certain things that members of the royal family simply do not do-because they are royalty. They do not say what they feel like, they do not go where they feel like, they do not do what they feel like doing because they have a standard to uphold and they understand their assignment and their worth.

I have come to learn that outside of my Lord, Jesus Christ, I am absolutely nothing, but all that I am is found in Him. In accordance with Acts 17:28 in Him we live, move and have our being. All that we are is in God. Before I understood that I was purchased with a ridiculously expensive price- the life of God's Son, I felt quite comfortable treating my body how I felt like treating it, doing what I wanted to do and going where I wanted to go. I was the 'god' of me, and as you read in earlier chapters, I did a pretty fine job of screwing things up. This was pure pride, nothing more and nothing less, but when I let go and let God be my God, things started to turn around for the better.

I was watching a movie the other day by the name of 'Overcomer' and in one particular scene, the star of the movie was led to Jesus and was directed to the book of Ephesians to understand who she was as a result of the decision that she made to give her life to The Lord. I thought this was such a powerful way to glean an understanding of what God's Word says that His sons and daughters are:

- Blessed with all spiritual blessings by God -Ephesians 1:3
- Chosen in Jesus before the foundation of the world – Ephesians 1: 4
- Predestinated to be adopted by Jesus – Ephesians 1:5
- Accepted into the beloved – Ephesians 1:6
- Redeemed by His blood and forgiven of our sins – Ephesians 1:7
- Heirs because of the inheritance – Ephesians 1:11
- Sealed with The Holy Spirit of Promise – Ephesians 1:13

There are many other Scriptures that speak to who we are in Jeesus, the following are just a few:
- Righteous in God – Romans 3:22
- A new creature in Christ – 2 Corinthians 5:17
- Saved by grace through faith -Ephesians 2:8

All that I am personally, is in God, on my own I am a hot mess. My identity is found in Him, it is who He says I am. If you ask me who I am today, my response would be that I am a daughter of the King of kings and everything that He says that I am. I am loved, I am accepted, I belong to Him, I am His and He is mine. Outside of Him, I am nothing and no-one, just a living soul and barely that.

I really wish that I could have come into this revelation sooner. If we do not understand who we are, we are a danger to ourselves, because we do not understand our value and worth and we would not treat our ourselves, the way that we need to. Further, we would set a higher standard for others to treat us the same way that we treat ourselves.

If we do not understand who we are, we will never fulfil our God-given purpose, the reason that God placed us on this earth in the first place. We did not just 'happen' to be here. It does not matter what our birth circumstances were, God created us for a reason. There is something that He has intentionally placed in us to fill a void in this earth and the longer we allow the enemy to deceive us into moving away from our true identity, the harder it becomes to fulfil this God-given purpose.

Who are you? What is your God-given purpose and assignment? God can take all of what you went through and still make a beautiful mosaic using every broken piece, if you allow Him to.

Chapter Eight: Stinking Thinking

As he thinketh in his heart, so is he... Proverbs 23:7

One of the things that I battled with and still have to be very intentional about is mind battles. This is one of the primary ways that the enemy has been attacking people for years, in their thoughts. One little seed of a thought, if left unchecked could bloom into full tree that directs a person's life. Unchecked thoughts can be almost like weeds that can choke out truth-if we allow it.

Everything starts with a thought, thoughts then influence desires, desires then influence actions, and actions attract consequences, whether good or bad. Thoughts are so important that in God's Word, He took time to tell us what we should be thinking about.

While we will talk about this in more detail later in the chapter, I want to share briefly on how 'stinking thinking' was a weapon that I succumbed to, more often that I would have preferred to. I did eventually learn how the enemy would plant words in my thoughts that would start a frenzy of mental activity, if I was not intentional about recognizing the trap.

The words 'always' and 'never' were some of these trigger words that helped me recognize that I was going down a 'rabbit hole' with my thoughts.

My husband, for example, would say something to me, and it would ignite a flurry of thoughts around what he said and how he said it. Before I knew it, I would be thinking things like – 'he never does this, or he always does that' and within moments I would be so angry at him that I stopped speaking. My husband, on the other hand would have no clue about what was going on with me and when we finally sat down to talk about it, I would realize just how far I let my thoughts go and lead me down the wrong path, over something that was likely very simple and could have easily been resolved had I just shut down that initial thought.

My journey has taught me that thoughts cannot be left alone, they must be constantly supervised, like little children. The reason that thoughts are so influential is because they are connected to the heart, and we are cautioned to guard our hearts because the issues of our very lives flow from it, in accordance with Proverbs 4:23.

This is also supported by Matthew 9:4 which says: "*And Jesus knowing their thoughts said, Wherefore think ye evil in your hearts?*" King James version. He knew their thoughts but he questioned why they were **thinking evil in their hearts**. I am understanding now why God told us to guard our hearts.

Sin is housed in the heart, even our decision to serve Jesus is a heart decision. In Matthew 15, Jesus said that the people drew to Him with their mouths but their hearts were far from Him. What happens in the heart matters to God, therefore we should not tolerate 'stinking thinking'!

Romans 12:2 says: "*And be not conformed to this world:* **but be ye transformed by the renewing of your mind,** *that ye may prove what is that good, and acceptable, and perfect, will of God.*" King James Version-emphasis added. We are transformed, our whole selves, when our minds are renewed! This verse alone tells us the power of a renewed mind. I have to pause to say that this renewal takes place when we allow God's Word to become rooted in our hearts, when we allow our lives to be directed by it, when we obey it, and by doing so, allow Jesus to be not only Savior, but Master and Lord.

2 Corinthians 10: 3-5 says: *"₃For though we walk in the flesh, we do not war after the flesh: ₄(for the weapons of our warfare are not carnal, but mighty through God to the pulling down of strong holds;) ₅casting down imaginations, and every high thing that exalteth itself against the knowledge of God, and <u>bringing into captivity every thought</u> to the obedience of Christ;"* King James version, emphasis added. This verse is perhaps one of the most direct verses with respect to our responsibility to govern our thought lives.

I heard a renowned Man of God- Apostle Joshua Selman teach a sermon that points out the fact that we are spiritual beings first, housed in earthly bodies and how spiritual life is. These verses mentioned above start off by reminding us that even though we live in the natural, what we are fighting is not natural and as a result, God has given us weapons that are not natural weapons either, but they are mighty and they are designed to attack and pull down the spiritual beings that we fight against. I often use this verse to remind me when people are fighting against me that its really not the person that I am at war with, but it is the spirit behind them, empowering them to fight against me. When I respond, I do not respond to the person, I respond to the spirit that is using them.

Verses 4 and 5 tell us that these weapons are 'mighty through God' to pull down strongholds. A stronghold is a fortified place[6] and it is not something that is easy to deal with, it requires a weapon that is much stronger to break it. With these God-given weapons we can not only cast down 'imaginations and every high thing' that tries to lift itself above what we know to be the truth about God and what He says, but these weapons allow us to bring our thoughts captive or under subjection and make them obey Jesus.

Let's talk about what this looks like practically. First, we will focus on the word 'captive'. Captive means 'kept within bounds or confined[7]'. Going back to my earlier example about my husband saying something to me, instead of allowing those thoughts to run around freely in my mind and grow into something bigger, if I hold these thoughts captive, I would keep them confined and disallow them from blossoming further by confronting them with the truth of God's Word.

I spent so many years of my life worrying and thinking about what others thought of me when I should have been seeking God's thoughts toward me, how my actions made **Him** feel, whether or not I offended **Him**. One day I was speaking with my Pastor-Apostle Lequient Bethel, and he was sharing a Scripture passage that really gripped him and as I read it, my heart was also gripped with conviction. The passage was found in Philippians 2:12 in the Amplified version- "So then, my dear ones, just as you have always obeyed [my instructions with enthusiasm], not only in my presence, but now much more in my absence, continue to work out your salvation [that is, cultivate it, bring it to full effect, actively pursue spiritual maturity] with awe-inspired fear and trembling [**using serious caution and critical self-evaluation to avoid anything that might offend God or discredit the name of Christ**]." Emphasis added.

This tugged at my heart because often I cared so deeply about what others thought and felt, to the extent that I altered my actions and decisions in order to avoid offending these people, who in some instances did not even have my best interests at heart, yet, God who created me and loves me so deeply can be offended by my actions. Not only this, sometimes our actions can discredit the name of Jesus. I never want to intentionally offend Father God, and this really made me think about the many ways that I casually treated God and I was really confronted and convicted by this Scripture.

Thoughts are so important to both God and to the enemy. In the Garden of Eden, Satan did not physically force Eve to disobey

God, he simply introduced a concept for her to consider, and the more she considered it, the more her perspective shifted and before she knew it, she was in a position that would cost her, her husband and their many descendants significant hardship and disconnection from God.

Isaiah 26:3 says: *"Thou wilt keep him in perfect peace, whose mind is stayed on thee: because he trusteth in thee."*- King James Version. If our minds are kept toward God, He promises to keep us in a place of perfect peace. This does not mean that we would not experience challenges, it does mean though, that in spite of these challenges God will be keep us in a state of perfect peace- once we keep our minds fixed on Him.

Philippians 4 has some very powerful wisdom and guidance for our thoughts. Life can feel like a lot sometimes and trust me, I have had many years when the battle in my mind raged and at the end of all of this 'stinkin thinkin' I was more upset, worried, and stressed than when I started thinking. I really could have experienced far less issues if I had managed my thought life better than I did. Philippians 4 starting from verse 6 say: *"Be careful for nothing; but in every thing by prayer and supplication with thanksgiving let your requests be made known unto God. 7And the peace of God, which passeth all understanding, shall keep your hearts and minds through Christ Jesus."* King James Version

Whenever we have challenges , we need to bring them to God in prayer. Tell Him what is happening and then ask Him for what we would like Him to do in order to resolve the issue, then thank Him. He didn't promise to follow our directives to the letter, but He did promise us once we do this His peace that does not even make sense, will keep not only our hearts but also our minds. Even if things turn out a different way, He will preserve us in His peace regardless of the outcome. In my first book- *The House That Faith Built*- I shared an experience where I had a very stressful situation that I presented to The Lord, and when I did, He did not answer the way I was expecting but to hear His response to me was enough to flood my heart with peace- I was able to rest in the assurance that He had me covered. In the end it worked out and God got all of the glory!

If this were not enough, God then told us what to think instead. In Philippians 4:8 God said "Finally, brethren, whatsoever things are true, whatsoever things are honest, whatsoever things are just, whatsoever things are pure, whatsoever things are lovely, whatsoever things are of good report; if there be any virtue, and if there be any praise, think on these things." This is such a beautiful reminder of where our thoughts ought to be, it is a 'litmus' test. Whenever we start to find ourselves heading down the rabbit hole of "stinkin thinking", we should first assess whether our thoughts are first and foremost true, then are they honest, then just, then pure, lovely, or a good report? Joyce Meyers put it this way- we have to think about what we are thinking about. In other words we have to assess our thoughts. This keeps the enemy out because it all starts with the mind.

If we are allowing the Word to transform our minds, we will have less and less instances of 'stinkin thinkin'.

Chapter Nine: Soul Ties

Human beings are comprised of three parts- body, soul and spirit. Our bodies are the only part of us that can be seen, and is tangible, the other parts that are unseen are the parts of us that are equally important. Like a plant with roots underground, our souls and spirits influence everything about us. Our everyday actions and decisions affect all three parts. What I am about to say is directly from what God has allowed me to learn over the years.

God is concerned about every part of us, and there is a role that every part of us plays. 1 Thessalonians 5:23 says *"And the very God of peace sanctify you wholly; and I pray God your whole spirit and soul and body be preserved blameless unto the coming of our Lord Jesus Christ."* King James Version. This distinctly outlines this principle of the whole man being comprised of three parts. In order to explain soul ties, it is necessary to start on this foundation.

Body
Our bodies are the only aspect of our triune beings that can be viewed with the natural eye. It is comprised of a series of systems that work together to keep us alive. As we are familiar with our bodies, I just want to make a few points that speak to God's expectations for our bodies.

1 Corinthians 6:19 says: *"What? know ye not that your body is the temple of the Holy Ghost which is in you, which ye have of God, and ye are not your own?"* King James Version. Our bodies are the temple or physical place where Holy Spirit resides, once we belong to God.

Permit me to divert for a moment- if you are expecting a house guest, you would do everything; in your power to ensure that your home is clean and organized and kept in a manner that impresses your house guest and makes them feel comfortable.

Now let's take this further and suppose that your house guest is a prominent person such as a king or president or even a celebrity. I'm sure that you would take this preparation to another level and do absolutely everything in your power to ensure that your guest of honor is not only comfortable but also given the very best that you have to offer. Now with this principle in mind, let's go back to this verse. Holy Spirit, a part of the only true Living God is not only the Guest but He is resident in your temple!

This in itself should tell us the importance of how we maintain our bodies, His temple. With this perspective we would always be mindful to keep these temples rested, free from foods and drinks that would harm us. We would be intentional on where we go, what we listen to, what we look at and even how we move around and exercise.

1 Corinthians 6:20 says: *"For ye are bought with a price: therefore glorify God in your body, and in your spirit, which are God's."* King James Version. Those of us who have surrendered our lives to Jesus have been purchased with a very costly price and our bodies and spirits ought to honor and glorify God. God gave us free wills, but when we give our lives to Him, we give up our wills for His will and that means that we simply cannot do whatever we want with what now belongs to God. Whatever we do, should bring Him glory!

Finally, Romans 12:1 says: *"I beseech you therefore, brethren, by the mercies of God, that ye present your bodies a living sacrifice, holy, acceptable unto God, which is your reasonable service."* King James Version. 'Beseech' means to 'beg for urgently or anxiously, or to request earnestly, This definition gives us insight into to the level significance of the point that Apostle Paul brought across. It is not just an urgent begging but a begging by the 'mercies of God'. Mercies is defined as compassion or forbearance (refraining from the enforcement of something that is due)[8].

I would like to stick a pin here. God is holy and He expects us to be holy, according to 1 Peter 1.16. Because He is holy, any sacrifice that we give Him should be an acceptable one, one that measures up to His standards. Imagine being given an opportunity to present a gift to a king. Would you give him just anything? I certainly would not. I would make sure that it is something that the king would want. Yet, unfortunately we sometimes give the King of kings anything, in any condition. This speaks volumes. When we revere and honor God, only our best will do.

The word 'sacrifice' means surrendering a possession as an offering to a deity[9] or, I would add, higher authority. So a living sacrifice means living a surrendered or a yielded life to God. To put it all together. It is imperative and critical that we surrender our bodies to God's Lordship in a way that is pure, pleasing and acceptable to God, this is the very least that we can do, He deserves nothing less.

Spirit

> "The burden of the word of the LORD for Israel, saith
> the LORD , which stretcheth forth the heavens, and
> layeth the foundation of the earth, and formeth the
> spirit of man within him"- Zechariah 12:1 KJV

God forms our spirits and this, in my view, is the part of us that He communicates with most. I am of this view based on what is said in the following verses:

The spirit of man is the candle of the LORD , Searching all the inward parts of the belly.- Proverbs 20:27 (KJV)

For what man knoweth the things of a man, save the spirit of man *which is in him? even so the things of God knoweth no man, but the Spirit of God.-* 1 Corinthians 2:11 (KJV)

As I stated earlier, we are first spiritual beings. It is very interesting that in Genesis 1:26, where Day 6 of creation was being described the Scriptures declare *"And God said, Let us make man in our image, after our likeness and let them have dominion over the fish of the sea, and over the fowl of the air, and over the cattle, and over all the earth and over every creeping thing that creepeth upon the earth.":*

John 4: 23-24 says: *"23But the hour cometh, and now is, when the true worshippers shall worship the Father in spirit and in truth: for the Father seeketh such to worship him. 24God is a Spirit: and they that worship him must worship him in spirit and in truth."*

So we see first that God decided to make man in His image and likeness, and the second Scripture tells us that God is a Spirit. It goes on to say that those who worship Him must worship Him in spirit and in truth. Note that the 's' is not capitalized, meaning with our **human** spirits.

I want to digress here for a moment and just put a plug in for worshipping God. Our spirit is our true selves, it is fully exposed to God and cannot be masked. Have you ever been around a stranger and within your spirit you felt disturbed even though you were not familiar with the person? What they said may have been one thing but what you felt in your spirit was not aligning with what the person said. In my culture we would say things like 'my spirit was crossed' or in other words 'my spirit was upset'. We would also say 'spirit knows spirit' and I have found it to be true. This means that our spirits are able to discern other spirits, whether they be good or bad.

So our spirit is a true reflection of us and it is from this place that worship of God must erupt, in order for it to be considered true worship. Worship is not about a melody or a song, it is when our spirits lift up honor, reverence and adoration to God.

But there is a spirit in man: And the inspiration of
the Almighty giveth them understanding.
Job 32:8 (KJV)

Soul

"And fear not them which kill the body, but are not able to
kill the soul: but rather fear him which is able to destroy
both soul and body in hell." – Matthew 10:28

The soul is the very core of who we are. It houses our emotions and is the part of us that remains when our body and spirit is done. 1 Corinthians 15:45 says: *"And so it is written, The first man Adam was made a living soul; the last Adam was made a quickening spirit."* King James Version

This Scripture provides insight into the fact that we are living souls, housed in human bodies with our spirits. The following Scriptures also give us insight into the depth of emotion that our souls can experience:

Job 30:25 (KJV)
Did not I weep for him that was in trouble? Was not my soul grieved for the poor?

Psalm 69:10 (KJV)
When I wept, and chastened my soul with fasting, That was to my reproach.

1 Samuel 1:10 (KJV)
And she was in bitterness of soul, and prayed unto the LORD , and wept sore.

2 Samuel 13:39 (KJV)
And the soul of king David longed to go forth unto Absalom: for he was comforted concerning Amnon, seeing he was dead.

Now that there is an understanding of the difference between the body, soul and spirit, let's talk about soul ties and why they play such an important role. The first mention of what is known as a soul tie is mentioned in 1 Samuel 18:1 which says: *And it came to pass, when he had made an end of speaking unto Saul, that the soul of Jonathan was knit with the soul of David, and Jonathan loved him as his own soul.*

In this passage, the souls of Jonathan, and David were 'knit' together and as a result Jonathan loved David the way he loved his own soul. This was a connection at the deepest levels. It is the connection that can be a good or bad thing. The soul tie between Jonathan and David was a good soul tie. They had a pure friendship, to the extent of brotherhood. Good soul ties can exist in friendships as well as marriages and other types of relationships.

One of the easiest ways, to develop a soul tie with someone is through sexual encounter. No sexual encounter is ever casual, regardless of how the world around us may explain it. Sex was designed to be between a husband and wife. Ephesians 5:31-32 says: *"For this cause shall a man leave his father and mother, and shall be joined unto his wife, and they two shall be one flesh. This is a great mystery: but I speak concerning Christ and the church."* King James Version.

When people connect sexually, they become one. What makes this so significant is that an access point is created between both persons and this tie has to be broken, in Jesus' Name, if it is not an appropriate connection. I have seen people in toxic, abusive relationships choose to stay with their abusers for years ,and one of the reasons that it is so hard for these people to disconnect is the presence of a soul tie. My first serious relationship, became emotionally abusive and it was very difficult to disconnect. Eventually I moved off of the island to get away from him, however the soul tie had to be disconnected before I was truly free from him.

There are also times when soul ties are developed in close, non-sexual relationships. A few years ago, I decided to leave the church that my family and I faithfully attended for 10 years. It was easier for me to walk away than my husband because he was very close to our pastor at the time. In fact they were so close, that they had formed an inordinate soul tie. Inordinate is defined as 'exceeding reasonable limits' or 'disorderly or unregulated'[10]. We ought to have boundaries for relationships and this soul tie had crossed these boundaries.

When people have these types of soul ties, there is often a level of influence that does not make sense. In my example, the words and influence of this particular pastor were more important to my husband than even our marriage. He could not see that healthy boundaries were crossed and our God ordained marriage was not as important as the words that this pastor spoke to him.

I recall petitioning the Lord to cut this soul time, and He told me that He had to carefully unravel the ties because if He cut them the way that I wanted Him to. I would lose my husband. In His faithfulness and mercy, this soul tie was eventually broken, and my husband left the church, some months after me and our children had already left.

I have even seen inordinate soul ties between parents and their children, where sons were so connected to their mothers that even if they dated women, their mothers would have more influence over the relationship than either of the participants of the relationship.

When a soul tie is not a healthy soul tie, it has to be broken. You may have repented to God for an inappropriate sexual relationship or even an unhealthy non-sexual relationship, however, while He will forgive you, according to His word, the tie must also be broken for you to be free of the impact of the soul tie.

If you have had these types of relationships, or even close toxic friendships where there are soul ties, it is very important to break these ties in Jesus' Name.

You may love Jesus, and be living a life according to His Word, but still be bound because you have not dealt with soul ties, or closed doors that were opened when you lived in sin.

I am not suggesting in any way that God is not able to break these ties, I am however noting that there are some things that we are required to do. God is the God of order and He never overrides our free will. Even in His absolute sovereignty, He honors our decisions and He honors legal rights. This means that if we have invited the enemy in, the enemy will have access rights until we tell him to leave. Even as we decide to get into inordinate relationships, we must decide to disconnect from them.

Let's now address how to break soul ties. Proverbs 18:21 says: *"Death and life are in the power of the tongue: And they that love it shall eat the fruit thereof."* King James Version. Our words have power and we can build and uproot with our tongues. Job 22:28 also says *"Thou shalt also decree a thing, and it shall be established unto thee: And the light shall shine upon thy ways."* King James Version.

Soul ties can be broken in faith by confessing the inordinate soul tie with each individual where this connection existed, repenting of it and seeking God's forgiveness then declaring in faith and asking God to break each soul-tie. Literally call the name of each person and ask God to break the soul-tie in the Mighty Name of Jesus.

There is nothing that is outside of God's scope and He has the capacity to disarm the powers of darkness. He is also willing to not only set us free, but make us free indeed, according to John 8:36.

Chapter Ten: Lessons That I Learned

Over the years, I tried so many things to numb the pain and loneliness in my life and nothing that I thought would work actually did, until I decided to surrender my life to Jesus. He shifted my life in ways that only He could have. I still had trials, I still had challenges and issues, but I had Jesus and He helped me to navigate much better than I ever could have on my own . He taught me about myself, and about Him and the fact that His love superseded anything that I could have ever done. He does not have limits to what He forgives for, He washes all sin and makes us completely whole.

My journey in God, was and still is an adventure, but one I would not trade for anything in the world. This journey is documented in my upcoming book called "The Dark Side of Religion" and while my walk with God has been quite interesting, I went through a process to learn the difference between being religious and having a relationship with God.

It still baffles me that this perfect God could love me, in spite of all of the wrong that I did in my life, He pursued me in spite of my flaws. Even in my walk with the Lord, I had to learn to let Him love me and teach me to love myself and forgive myself.

Our missteps and mistakes are only failures if we do not learn from them. Over the years, I have learned many lessons, some that I initially considered failures but I eventually realized that God used these mistakes to develop character in me and to mature me.

In this final chapter, I want to share some of these lessons that I learned along the way with you. It is my hope and prayer that you are able to also learn from these lessons and that they will help you to take that first step on your journey of healing.

Lesson 1

As I stated at the very beginning, this book was a struggle for to write. As I wrote though, a particular Scripture kept ringing in my spirit- Luke 9:24 which says *"For whoever desires to save his life will lose it, but whoever loses his life for My sake will save it."* New King James Version. There are many who know about me who think that I have the perfect life, and the perfect marriage and children and that I have it all together. I am who I am only because of the grace that God has extended to me.

As you would have read, my life was and actually still is far from perfect. This book has brought me to a place of vulnerability that I never expected to share publicly, this Scripture reminds me that through losing I actually gain. This brings me to the first lesson - **We lose nothing worth keeping when we obey God.**

I had started to share my story in snippets with others, and I realize that the more that I share, the easier it is becoming to share. I have also come across people who experienced the exact same things that I did and I realize that in 'losing' my own life and reputation it has allowed God to use me to help others to heal.

Lesson 2

We often project our relationship with our earthly father on our relationship with God and when I learned this, I realized why it was so difficult for me to connect with God and for me to comprehend the love that He has for me. It was hard to imagine a Father whose love was not based on how I behaved, or what I did or accomplished. My earthly father was not in my life very long and while it was not his fault that he died prematurely, this void caused me to struggle with a spirit of abandonment.

Years later I learned that he was not as wonderful of a person that I thought he was and I began to understand the hatred that my grandparents had for him, yes, they loathed him, and projected these feelings on my brother and I- which in itself perpetuated feelings of abandonment and rejection. This brings me to lesson 2- **my Heavenly Father cannot be compared to my earthly father.** Even if my dad was perfect, he could never measure up to God. God's love is not based on who I am, it is based on His own goodness, kindness, mercy, and most of all- His own character. Love is not just what He does, it is who He is!

Lesson 3

This lesson is actually related to my second point. It does not matter what we have done, how many people we have been intimate with, how many times we did things to hurt ourselves, how many stupid decisions we made, how many times we failed or fell down, how drunk we got, how many times we got horrible grades, cursed people out, cursed ourselves out, how much drugs we took and the list can go on, God loves us, I mean really loves us. His love is almost impossible to comprehend.

I now understand what the Psalmist meant when he said Psalms 8:4 *"what are mere mortals that you should think about them, human beings that you should care for them?"* New Living Translation. So this lesson is the fact that **God loves us, period. There are no strings attached.**

While this may be something others always knew, I always performed to try to get the attention and the love of others and now knowing that God loves me has lifted a heavy burden. I don't have to be anything other than who I already am, I don't have to try to please others, I just want to please Him, not because He will love me any more than He does already, but because He deserves my love in return for all of who He is and His love for me.

Lesson 4

Lesson four is that **I am already equipped with what I need**. Like a seed that has everything that it needs to flourish into a tree with fruits, God has put everything that I need for the path that He chose for me inside of me already. I am who I am, I do not have to strive to be anything or anyone else. **I am sufficient, I am enough.**

It took me what feels like forever to understand this, and this too was enlightening and liberating. I do not have to work hard on trying to get what God has already given me. I do, however, have a responsibility to steward it, to nurture it and to make sure that it gives Him a return on His investment in me.

In the Parable of the Talents in Matthew 25 verses 14 though 25, Jesus spoke about a Master who entrusted three servants with money that was in proportion to the abilities that they had. When the master came back, he asked the three servants to tell him what they did with what was entrusted to them.

To the two servants who made a return on what was given to them, he celebrated them, but to the one who simply gave the master back what was originally given him without any return on it, he was called "*wicked*", "*slothful*" and "*condemned*".

Notice that they were given money in proportion to abilities that they already had. We are each entrusted with abilities from God and He expects us not to sit on them, but to multiply what He has given us. I can do it, because He blessed me according to the abilities that He has given me- so can you based on what He has given you!

Lesson 5

This fifth lesson is one about disappointment and one that was mentioned earlier in this book. God is God all by Himself! He is a jealous God and He does not tolerate anything or anyone who wants to be raised up as a god in His place. My husband, my children, my job, my finances, my car, my mom, not even me can replace God in my life. **Anytime I placed my expectations anywhere other than God, I was disappointed**. Proverbs 29:25 in the New Living Translation says: *"Fearing people is a dangerous trap, but trusting the LORD means safety."* God placed people in our lives for many reasons, but not one of those reasons point to any person replacing God in our lives. Yes- honor people, love people and respect them but never put them in God's place.

I had a very good friend and sister that I looked up to almost to the point of reverence. I loved her wholeheartedly and I revered her if I could be honest. She had such a pure walk with the Lord and I admired it to the point of idolatry. The Lord allowed me to witness her go through a season of falling apart and this person who I thought was as perfect an example as any could be, crumbled before me and started to behave in a manner that was shocking for me.

I was hurt, really hurt, disappointed and confused. She later got back on track, and came back stronger, but this was a powerful lesson for me. God showed me her humanity. We have since reconciled our relationship but I have put her in her proper place in my life, a sister yes, but not as a god. **God's place belongs to Him alone!**

Lesson 6

All that I need is in God! This lesson was such a profound one for me. I looked for so many things that I thought that I needed, and even when I got the things that I worked so hard to get, I never felt fulfilled.

God has such a profound sense of what we need and if we would only take the time to trust Him, rest in Him and in His love for us, we would realize that many of the things that we are chasing do not bring fulfillment. He can bring solutions to us in an instant if we would pause long enough to listen.   There is nothing that we can achieve in this life that we can take with us when we die.

Growing up I would always hear my mom say that only what is done for Christ will last and I am starting to understand why she kept saying this. Do not get me wrong, we do not work for salvation, it is a gift from God, we do not have to work to be loved or accepted by God- we are loved and accepted and chosen. I am not talking about 'dead works' – I share more on this concept in my book *"The Dark Side of Religion"*, I am speaking about the focus of our hearts on treasures that last beyond this earth.

In Matthew 6, starting at verse 19 Jesus said: *"Don't store up treasures here on earth, where moths eat them and rust destroys them, and where thieves break in and steal. 20Store your treasures in heaven, where moths and rust cannot destroy, and thieves do not break in and steal. 21**Wherever your treasure is, there the desires of your heart will also be**."* New Living Translation- Emphasis added.

Our heart's desires should not be for material things that do not last, our hearts should be fixed on Jesus and on living in a way that brings glory to Him alone.

Lesson 7

I learned, and I continue to learn that **I am not nor can I ever be perfect. While I am not perfect, I am in fact righteous and this is not because of anything that I could have possibly done on my own, but because of Jesus!** I learned this powerful lesson and this governs me and keeps me assured of my right-standing with God. 1 Corinthians 5:21 says: *"For God made the only one who did not know sin to become sin for us, so that we might become the righteousness of God through our union with him."* The Passion Translation.

I will also squeeze another lesson in lesson seven and that is that **I am not condemned.** This is a tool that the enemy uses to place a weight on many Christians. Romans 8:1 says: *"There is therefore now no condemnation to them which are in Christ Jesus, who walk not after the flesh, but after the Spirit."* King James Version.

The story of my life, in my mind anyway, was one of condemnation and guilt, feeling condemned for everything that I had done but I cannot begin to say how grateful I am that Jesus took on the penalty for every sin that I committed, of which there ave been many, in order to reconcile me to God. This is a demonstration of the love and commitment of God. He saved us from our sins, clothed us in His righteousness and liberated us from the weight of sin and condemnation! Hallelujah!

Lesson 8

I can have as much of God as I want. It is crazy how I envied people who I know walked closely with The Lord, not even realizing that that I could be just as close or even closer because God is just as available to me as He is to anyone else.

James 4:8 says: *"Draw nigh to God, and he will draw nigh to you. Cleanse your hands, ye sinners; and purify your hearts, ye double minded.*" King James Version. All I have to do is draw close to Him and He will come close to me. This lesson sounds simple but it is really a game changer. God wants to be close to us, He gave up His whole Son, His only begotten child so that we could come close to Him. He wants to speak to me more than I want Him to speak to me, He wants to be closer to me, He wants covenant relationship and He is willing to wait patiently, woo me, pursue me gently, call out to me to draw me to Himself. He is so patient, He is such a Gentleman, His intentions and motives are so pure, He just loves me so much and He feels the exact same way about each of us. He can give each of us His undivided attention at the same time.

We do not have to look around at what He is doing in the lives of others, all we have to do is come closer to Him, seek Him out, make time for Him, talk to Him, take time to listen to Him, study His Word to understand His Heart and His character and allow Him to lead us. It is crazy how even the smallest details of our lives He is concerned about!

I heard a warning sound the other day in my car, and this car was, at the time of writing, seventeen years old. The dashboard messages did not work but I could still hear the warning ringing out even though I could not see what the warning was for. I heard the Holy Spirit gently telling me to check my oil. When I pulled into the gas station, the issue was in fact my oil and it had dropped to dangerously low levels. God is concerned! He didn't want me to break down on the roadside with my daughter in the car and my other daughter waiting for me at school to pick her up. That may sound simple to you but it was such a wonderful reminder to me that there is no detail that He is not concerned about!

Lesson 9

This lesson is outlined in 1 Samuel 15:22 –"*And Samuel said, Hath the LORD as great delight in burnt offerings and sacrifices,* **As in obeying the voice of the LORD? Behold, to obey is better than sacrifice, And to hearken than the fat of rams.**" King James Version – Emphasis added. This was a very tough lesson for me- **to obey God**.

As a parent now, it is abundantly clear how important it is for my children to obey me when I speak to them, it could literally be a matter of life and death. I may not always explain why they should obey me but it does not negate the fact that I expect them to do so because it is in their best interests.

God is a parent on a much grander scale and **when He tells me to do something or not to do something it is always for my good.** He can see the end of all things before they even begin. I may not always understand and I do not have to- my obedience, however, is critical and can mean the difference between life or death!

As I near the end of this book I am beginning to see more of the reasons that God had me to write this book. I know that this book will bring healing to many because of what He told me, but this book was the method that God chose to heal me. This journey of healing was years in the making and as I journey back into my past I was able to cry through things that impacted my life, even from I was a little girl.

My mom, at the time of writing, was suffering from dementia and while I am not a scientist, I earnestly believe that she is suffering for two reasons, one was a generational curse that needed to be broken and the other is the secrets and the pain that she kept in her heart and never exposed to to anyone or to God for healing. She kept it inside. James 4:16 says: "*Confess your faults one to another, and pray one for another, that ye may be healed. The effectual fervent prayer of a righteous man availeth much.*"

Opening up, expecially about places of deep wounding, is not easy, by any stretch of the imagination. It allows us though to release it instead of mulling over it and allowing the enemy to trap us in dangerous cycles of condemnation and guilt.

Jesus told us that we shall know the truth and the truth sets us free (See John 8:32). I recently spoke with a colleague who told me that her mother witnessed the murder of her own father and she had to leave her home as a child to escape with her mother by boat to another country to be free. As an adult now, her mother recently started to become delusional and she started going outside with her bags packed waiting for a boat and when it never shows up she would go back inside disappointed. My heart was broken for her as she spoke about her mother's sudden illness and I realize that it is the trauma of her past that caused her mind to break because it was never exposed and dealt with.

When I started to embark on the journey of healing, I started to see a therapist and she shared the concept of 'stuffing' with me- just putting things aside almost like in a closet and one day it will eventually overflow if we do not go back to declutter. I am saying all of this to say it is imperative that no matter what, we obey God- even if it hurts.

Lesson 10

So while there are many more lessons that I have learned along this journey called life I will wrap this chapter up by sharing one last one- **never lose confidence in God!** Faith is having confidence in who God is, and who He is has nothing to do with anything that we experience. We may feel lonely but that does not take away His ability to bring us to bring us to a place of acceptance, a place of fellowship, a place of peace. We may experience lack, but that does not take away His ability to provide and to shift things in an instant and bring us to a place of abundance.

God may not give us what we want all of the time or at any time for that matter, but it does not make Him any less God than He already is. He is sovereign, holy, righteous, perfect, and the best Father ever. His love is unconditional, His motives are always pure and even when our confidence in our own selves wavers, our confidence in Him should never waver.

I have taken many side streets to get to the path that God chose for me, I could have taken the easy route but He allowed my missteps to teach me and to shape me, I can stand now saying that He is a healer, because He healed me, He is a deliverer, because He delivered me, He is a provider, because He provided for me, He is the Father to the fatherless because he fathers me. If I had a perfect life I could only tell you these things from a distance, from someone else's perspective, but I can actually share from my own perspective.

When I gave my life to the Lord at the age of 11 and I backslid so many times after, I had no idea that years later, in the midst of rebellion, Jesus would use a co-worker to share a song – Be Blessed by Yolanda Adams- to bring me back to Him. She simply said I want you to listen to this song and as I sat down and listened I just remember tears rolling down my face, God used this song to minister to me in the mi

dst of all of my mess and I surrendered and never looked back. This was more than seventeen years from the time of me writing this book. Even that song spoke to God's character! Things may not work out for you the way you may want or hope, but rest assured that in Him, He will always cause things to work out in your best interests. Never lose hope, never give up, He can give you peace in the most disturbing of situations and He can and will heal you if you allow Him to.

KANDI CASH

Conclusion

I have heard the saying many times, "healing is not a destination, it is a journey", and a very necessary one. As I walk this journey, I am learning more and more that God can make something beautiful out of the ugliest of moments and situations. I have learned to love myself, flaws and all, I have learned how to forgive, and the importance of forgiving, I have learned how to endure and how to mature.

I look back and I am amazed at what God has done and what He continues to do in my life. He is using my story for His glory and I am ok with that. He has given me a heart of compassion and a heart for those who, like me, have experienced rejection and brokenness. He has made me living proof that He can put all of the broken pieces together and make a beautiful masterpiece out of these shattered pieces. This masterpiece has nothing to do with anything that I have done other than allow Him in to heal me.

Healing is a choice that we must make in order to move toward it. Many, like I did for many years, recognize their brokenness but for whatever reason, choose to stay in that place and not move forward.

Once a decision is made to heal, we have to be committed to go all the way. Many times I would start a process and then stop- the pain of my past was so much for me to bear. At times I would even be immobilized by fear, what people would think, what people would say, how would people would view me. I realize now that these were tactics of the enemy to keep me bound and to keep me from releasing my testimony for myself and others- we overcome by the Blood of the Lamb and the word of our testimony (See Revelation 12:11).

Obeying God is more important to me than my reputation and I am so grateful that He entrusted me with this testimony.

I don't know where you are or what your story is, but I encourage you to let Jesus heal your heart, sit with Him and let Him lead you down your path of healing. This path may be like mine- writing a book, or it may be going back to apologize to someone, it may be making a decision to forgive that person who shattered your innocence, it may be forgiving your parents or just writing a letter. Whatever it is, do it- not just for you, but for yourself, your children, your spouse or for those that God has connected to you and to your story.

I would like to end the way I started – with a prayer.

Father,
I present the person reading this book now and I ask that you
awaken a desire deep within them to be healed and to be set free.
I ask that you remove the temporary bandages that they have placed
on their hearts and allow them to become vulnerable before You so
that You can touch them and bring them into complete wholeness.

Father, I ask that you give them the strength to walk through
healing and on those days when they feel like giving up, I
pray that You would lovingly gather them in Your arms
and carry them and give them Your strength.

Father ,I break every word curse over their lives, every generational
curse that kept them in cycles. I decree and declare whom the Son
sets free is free indeed and I thank You that this is their portion-
freedom and I thank You for it in Jesus' mighty and matchless Name!
Amen

Epilogue

On the evening of March 27th, 2024, I walked into my mother's room to get her prepared for bed. She had quite a bit of cold in her throat for a few days before and it sounded bad to the point where I decided to nebulize her so that her throat could be cleared and she could sleep without issues. I nebulized her and cleared her mouth and lay her on her side. I was tired, and a little annoyed at her stubbornness for holding on to the liquid in her mouth. I would usually tell her goodnight, and tell her that I love her. I honestly don't remember if I did this particular night.

I stayed up for a little while longer to watch something that my youngest daughter insisted on me watching and finally got to bed. When I woke up the following morning, it was still dark and I got dressed to clean my mom up before I got ready for work. Oddly enough the two prior mornings, I was almost completely dressed before I remembered I had to get my mom cleaned up. This had never happened to me before. On the morning of March 28 2024, however, I was very intentional about making sure that I did not forget to get mom cleaned up before getting dressed the way I did the two previous mornings.

I walked into her room and met her laying on her side, the way I left her before, but something was very different. She was very still and very quiet. I looked at her and did not see the usual pulsating movement in her neck. I leaned a little closer to listen to her back for her breathing, but I heard nothing. I rolled her over to look at her and she had a very strange look on her face. Her eyes were open and she just had a blank stare. I remember pushing her eyelid down expecting it to bounce back up and for her to blink like she usually would when she slept with her eyes open. Her eyelids however stayed shut.

I ran to get my husband, who was still in bed, and he came in the room, walked over to Mom and looked back at me, nodded and told me that she was gone.

A wave of emotions swept over me, after more than fifteen years of suffering dementia, that was it, and my mother was finally at rest. I am not unfamiliar with pain or even grief, but this was different.

My mother knew Jesus and loved Him and all I wanted to know was whether or not she saw Him. Sometime later that day, my husband came to me quietly and released a Word from The Lord that He had ministered to Him, that like His Son rose in glory after Good Friday, so will she. I can't begin to describe the relief and peace that I felt, knowing that in His infinite mercy, God responded to little old me. He later confirmed with another friend that I could grieve with hope, knowing that if I live for Him, I will see her again.

There is a point to this life, and there is a reason for everything that we go through. We may not understand it, and we may certainly not like the process, but God is able to give us beauty for ashes and joy for sorrow. He is also able to take what is broken and make a beautiful masterpiece out of it, if we let Him. I am grateful for this healing journey, grateful that God started it before He allowed my mother to transition. I am grateful that He prepared my heart, and I am grateful that He prepared this path for me.

Healing is in fact a journey, and not a destination, and my prayer is that as you embark on, or even continue your journey, that you would do so knowing that each day gets better and one day, you will understand the point of it all, and hopefully you will see the many others that you have helped along the way, just because you decided to take that bold step toward your healing journey,

This is my story, and this is the truth about me. May God bless you and heal you.

---

[1] www.missiondelafe.org
[2] Source Mirriam Webster Dictionary
[3] Source Mirriam Webster Dictionary
[4] Source: Merriam-Webster Dictionary
[5] Source: Merriam-Webster Dictionary
[6] Source: Merriam Webster Dictionary
[7] Source: Merriam Webster Dictionary
[8] Source: Merriam Webster dictionary
[9] Source: Oxford dictionary
[10] Source: Merriam Webster Dictionary

Acknowledgement

I am grateful to God for His absolute mercy and grace, I acknowledge Him first and foremost for always keeping me and blessing me with His love. I love you Daddy!

I want to also thank my husband for his patience with me during this process.I love you sir.

I want to send a special thank you to my dear friend and sister Ashquel who was kind enough to proof-read this book and share her very profound insights.

I would also like to thank my Apostle, brother and friend, Lequient Amore Bethel for his wisdom and for writing such a beautiful foreword, and designing my book cover.

I would like to thank my very small circle of friends who encouraged me to keep going.

To my Pastor Cam Rolle and Revival U family, I love you all.

Finally, I would like to thank you, for going along on this journey of healing with me. May God continue to grant you grace and peace.